LANDING

LANDING

Reflections on Breakups and Yearning

MOLLY FRANCES

To Frank, my feline son whose loyalty and affection remains steadfast despite the separation from his human father who dutifully fed him every morning for years.

Contents

ADVISING

GROWING

LANDING

Introduction

I spent eight years sharing my life with a beautiful man, J. We were young when we first got together—him at 19, me at 21. We said goodbye at 27 and 29. We parted ways in January 2023, agreeing mutually that our story together had finished. I had moved back to Connecticut from California to live with my family in November 2022 after 18 months of brewing realization that I was, honestly, lost. I had no direction, and the vision I was forming for my life seemed increasingly incompatible with my relationship.

I have chosen to not write extensively about the relationship itself, and instead primarily focus this writing on my own internal experience. What I will say about our relationship is that the love we shared was very real. We both were committed to each other's stability and contentment. We laughed together and we built a language of our own. We had nicknames—mine for him was *dof*, his for me was *mol*. We were affectionate and accommodating, and we did not ever want to hurt each other. We had running gags, made up songs, rituals and enjoyed many adventures. We shared a great love of food and enjoyed exploring new restaurants together.

The relationship was a safe one. It was something comfortable to come home to. I once wrote about him that he is "something more holy than most," and I still believe it. He was a lovely partner, and the woman he will one day spend his life with will be extremely fortunate to have found him, and the type of romance he himself craves will bloom with the right woman also. We just were not *it* for each other in the end.

A break up is as long as the relationship; the ending comes with the beginning. Something my ex told me on our final day together was that he felt this was always how our story would end, like there was an inevitable pull of fate that led us to it. I believe that's true. I think of it like the human life; from the moment we are born we begin to die. Various parts of our love developed and grew, reached a peak, and gradually declined. We reached a point where we decided to celebrate the life we built together by letting it dissolve into memory. Love can be long-term and stable and still come to a natural endpoint.

These writings are a compilation of personal narrative and reflective essays about breaking up and rediscovering what you truly want. They are a bit of an emotional roller coaster, as break ups are. The writing is organized into five sections; Leaving, reflections on ending my relationship of eight years; Yearning, reflections on what I want from love in the future; Advising, advice for others considering or going through breakups; Growing, reflections on a turning point after reconnecting with my ex; and Landing, an epilogue about coming down to earth.

Leaving

February 13, 2015 / after Rilke and the mill

I am imagining our love as fire,
that your love ignites a fire in mine.
It is a flame without the quality of fervor that sets ablaze forests
or of immediacy as when a match meets gasoline.
It is flame on a log: burning slowly at first,
with some effort (perseverance perhaps)
then slowly encapsulating the wood entirely.
The fire blazes safely in a hearth,
a place for friends, family, lovers to gather—
reflecting, considering, remembering, wishing,
and taking comfort in each other's arms
(a warm fire exactly where love intended it to be)

I must stay

It is January 5th, 2023. I am stewing, marinating in respiratory illness and madly fixated on perfecting a draft of a travel memoir about my trip to Ireland last fall. I told my mom earlier that my spirit feels stuck; due to being sick I have not moved enough. There is energy caught in my body that needs to shift. My period came today. This helped somewhat.

This morning I sat up in bed and wept, clenching my chest for ten minutes. This fit of emotion emerged suddenly, overpowering all other thought and sensation, seizing my full attention. I knew when I finished crying I'd begun to bleed, and I was correct. This is my rhythm. I wonder how many more months of this gift until I lose it, my most direct reflection of God, my ability to create new life. I wonder if I have the gift at all. I suppose I've never tried.

On New Year's Eve, J folded napkins for my mother. She had a stack of fifty and no idea how to fold them. He searched for a tutorial on YouTube and got to work. At the sight of this kindness, I was overcome by guilt-laden sorrow so great I could not bear it. I tried to zone out on my phone, but the weight cracked through my dissociative scrolling. I had to simply *feel*.

I went into the closet-sized half-bathroom in my parents' room. I looked in the mirror and asked myself what hurts. I am lonely. I do not understand it. I am wanting. I can't understand for what, other than a fantasy. I feel feral, like my heart and womb are clawing out-ward aching for something in a haze, searching through a blackened cave I cannot see through. I say it is God I must be after, it is always God. I close my eyes and shake my head, descending rapidly into quiet sobs. I beg Him to take this away, or to bring me what I want, whatever that is, if I'm meant to have it.

I close my eyes and pray to see a future beyond this pain, a pain I have been feeling near-constantly at varying levels of intensity for over a year, against which my attempts to control and avoid have become futile. My mind is dark for a moment, then a vision flashes: a breeze through an open door, arms around my waist and a kiss on my neck, cooking, somewhere quiet and hidden, a tablecloth and flowers. I can't see where, or who, or when. It's just a daydream any-way. I lean my head against the windowsill to cry. I don't know how to get there, if it could ever be. I don't understand if this is what I want, but this is a hunger deeper than my stomach yearns to be fed. I look in the mirror and breathe. My face does not look teary, no redness. No one will know I've been crying.

I calm down and return to the kitchen. J has finished folding the napkins. I admire the broad width of his shoulders and his comfortable posture. I love the jeans he's wearing today. His beard is perfectly groomed, as always. What is wrong with me that such a beautiful man, with a devoted, patient heart, is someone I want to leave? Who else could put up with me? Who else could love me like he does? Who else would fold my mother's napkins? It is a small thing, but that is exactly what I anguish over not being able to simply accept as *enough*: dutifully kind, earnestly willing, unas-sumingly generous. Why is this not enough? There is nothing wrong with J. There must be something wrong with me.

Two nights ago my mother invited me to spend an hour reading with her. I lit a fire in the fireplace in our basement pub and added a block of turf. She poured us wine. I read the book that found me in

Maine in small bookstore on my birthday. J and I shared a birthday, and to celebrate, we booked a cabin in the woods near the shoreline in Georgetown, Maine. We were completely alone together, and I felt like an island.

On the morning of our birthday, I was texting a friend about my future visions—in this case, one day having a cottage by the sea in Ireland and a cabin in the woods in Maine—and he mocked them in a way I had expected. He poked fun at the environmental wastefulness of it, a viewpoint which I find eyeroll-inducing, but can tolerate from a friend. I told J, expecting laughter, but he agreed with the criticism. A dam burst. This was a point of no return.

"I don't care if this other person thinks my future dreams are frivolous, but *you* are supposed to want them with me. You are my life partner. You are the person who I'm supposed to be discovering and building these dreams with."

"Molly, I don't know if *you* want your future dreams with *me*. Do you even see me in them? You need to figure that out. I don't know how else we can keep going if you haven't figured that out."

My anger faded and my stomach dropped. I went quiet and dropped down onto the couch. He sat next to me and I began to cry. I knew the answer, but I could not bear it.

Later in the day, we went to a bookstore in Brunswick. I decided I would browse book covers, to compare the design I had drafted for a book I was writing. J and I were having a pleasant time together, but under the surface I was brooding about the status of our relationship and my own lack of direction. I prayed to God to show me where I need to be going next. About five minutes later, just as I decided to check out and leave the store, a book caught my eye. It was tucked away, laying on the shadowed corner of a tier below a main display surface, somewhat obscured. *In Kiltumper: A Year in an Irish Garden.* I picked it up and was bowled over by eerie, shocking synchronicity.

The book is the memoir of a couple who, in their 20s, left the eastern US to move to the west coast of Ireland, in County Clare, to become writers and raise a family. The back cover reads that it teaches "about darkness and stars, about sunlight and silence, about things out of your control." The inside flap describes it as "a meditation on the power, beauty, and importance of the natural world."

I swear I am writing the prequel to this book. The description of their life is, down to the location in County Clare, my very dream. These themes are at the core of my own story, the memoir I'd been writing, down to the darkness and the stars, the very thing that led me to my yearning for the night sky in that same Irish county. A desire for a life like theirs led me to where I am right now.

I've made slow progress reading their book since I purchased it. It has been a few weeks, and I am now halfway through it, reading about the month of July. The book is a bit slow-moving, unhurried like the rhythms of their rural life. I come to a passage reflecting on how it's "one thing to dream a life, another to try and live it."

The paragraph reads, "What is required is a level of faith. First, you have to believe that a life like this is worth living. That it is what you should be doing. I mean 'you' in the narrowest sense, I'm not being prescriptive, not for one instant advocating that this is what anyone else should be doing. It is too hard for one thing. Not everyone can be this lucky is another. And another, even more rare, that it requires two to have the same shared vision, and, importantly, accept the consequences."

it requires two to have the same shared vision, and, importantly, accept the consequences.

it requires two to have the same shared vision

the same shared vision

The vision that I have, that I do not share with J. I lay the book down and rest my head against my hand. I want to cry. Their partnership is what I have been yearning for. This is what I've let slowly take hold of my spirit over the last year. I put words to this wanting in June 2022, and it has seized control over my decision-making ever since. When I found the book in Maine, I chose to take it, sincerely, as a sign I was on the right path if I would only have the courage to keep walking. I reflect back on the words I wrote in June:

"What I want, deeply, desperately, is some kind of creative partnership with a person whose vision, values and creative passions align with mine."

The words in the book read like a direct response to my own writing. It has been a year of strange coincidences, and here is one more. Wisdom from an aged married pair who have lived my exact dream, in a memoir they've written together. After all my honesty about my desire, my choice to leave my life in California, this feels like a cosmic taunt from God. I read the whole paragraph over and over. *Even more rare.* The wine seeps into my blood as I exhale the hope from my body. *Not everyone can be this lucky.* I zone out on the cover of the book, drained of my audacity.

I will never find him who shares my vision, because he does not exist. I have someone who loves me, and it is delusional to want anything more. I cannot chase a daydream. I must stay.

With softness, acceptance, let go

On January 13, 2023, I flew to California to pack up my belongings in the apartment that my boyfriend and I shared for four years. As soon as I stepped foot inside, every fiber of my being told me to leave. I looked around. None of this was mine anymore. Our collage, our memories, they are in the past. My clothes, my books, our puzzles. The games I bought him for Christmas we never found the inspiration to play, Sherlock Holmes still in its plastic wrap, Bruxelles only thumbed through to look at the art.

In my distance and dejection, a memory stirred of my time in Ireland in August 2022. J and I spent a weekend in a cozy cottage in Doolin, a town on the west coast. We stood outside on a cloudy, windy night after driving back from a traditional music session in a pub. The wind enveloped me, sinking into my nerves and cradling my eager spirit. I felt my heart soften and my body lighten, then I arrived at a deep, uncomfortable knowing. Earlier that day after praying the rosary, I had the revelation that I must return to Connecticut. Now, I knew something more frightening, a truth I had been running away from for a long time: *You need to let go of J.* I could not turn back from this, but I tried. I wanted to will myself to continue making the decision I had been making for eight years: Stay; do not succumb to your restless yearnings.

The following night in Doolin, we went to listen to music. I was consumed again by confusion and fear, tinged with frustration. I could not understand it, but I wished I was alone. He was so loving, so happy to be by my side, and yet I wanted this all to myself. I felt guilty. I prayed. *What is wrong with me? What am I supposed to do?* My attention immediately returned to the music in the pub. The band was playing a Bob Dylan cover.

The answer, my friend, is blowing in the wind
The answer is blowing in the wind

My mind flashed to the night prior, the knowing that I must leave. I closed my eyes and prayed for anything, any answer but this one. I asked my reason to overpower my pattern-seeking and narrative-weaving. I shoved this memory away.

On the afternoon of my first day back in Santa Cruz, five months after the memories in Ireland, I texted my best friend Emily about my confusion. I recounted this anecdote from Ireland, which I had recalled only after reading a note in my phone where I had journaled about it. She called me and we talked for an hour.

"Molly, J is an amazing guy, but you have tried to reframe your relationship over and over again and it hasn't worked. We've been having this conversation since you moved out there in 2018. So many people would love what you guys have, but it sounds like *you* don't, and that is all that matters. You also mentioned a memory about being in Ireland, where you were outside writing and praying, and he was inside doing housework.

The thing is, that's perfect for so many people. They want some-one who will be more of a stabilizing force, who doesn't mind the drudgeries, so that they can go off and be a creative free spirit on their own. You don't want that. You want someone to be outside being creative with you."

My reason synced up with my intuition, finally. She was right. I knew I would need to tell him this. I knew, finally, I had to face the truth. This relationship, as loving as it was, must reach its conclusion. Our storyline had come to an end.

*****

Truthfully, as soon as I returned to California to pack up the apartment, I felt resentment for him. This was part of how I *knew*. Resentment is relational rot, and I realized it was too deep to mend—and it was unfair for him to receive. Earlier in the day, before my call with Emily, I tried to will myself to stop feeling it, as I always did. We were getting mildly frustrated with each other as we handled the logistics of moving. On the drive back from a store, I tried managing my frustration and disconnect by suggesting something fun: *Let's roll down the windows and put on music and drive around for a while. We can keep packing later, we could use a break.*

He immediately said no, he didn't want to. I felt furious, as if someone had pulled me by a leash into a cage and slammed the door in my face. I wanted to shout at him or jump out of the car. I knew this was, of course, a wildly disproportionate response to a *no*. Often such a suggestion would be met with eager agreement. Instead of saying anything, I merely rolled up the windows and sat silently until we got home.

It was a minor exchange, but it seemed to be a perfect example of our incompatibility. I could not fault or condemn him for this peculiarity of our chemistry, and he never did it intentionally—in fact, I believe he often intended to do just the opposite. It was due to no inherent shortcoming of his, but merely a fact of how our personalities found harmony and dissonance in each other. I chose him for the same reason I decided to leave him: His influence restrained my passion and restricted my impulses.

**

The evening after my phone call with Emily, J and I decided to drive down to Monterey to get dinner. The whole drive, I felt a knot in my stomach. I knew I had to follow through on what I had decided earlier in the day. It was as if I would be delivering news of a death, but the timing was not yet right. I was carrying around this brutal secret the second half of the day as he went about like nothing had changed.

Halfway through our meal, I told him about the conversation with Emily. We went back and forth—maybe we should try a break? No, there's no point. We're either done or we're not. But maybe, maybe it's worth keeping the door open.

We talked about the justification for ending things. Do we even want kids together? No. We couldn't see ourselves agreeing on child rearing. I said I'd want them to be at least exposed to Catholicism, and he was adamantly against it. Neither of us knew where we'd be in a year's time. Why put this off any longer?

After an hour, the agreement was reached. We were both done. We were both aching for something else. I think it was the first time he had acknowledged that to himself. He said more than this, but what I remember included: *I want someone who cares about my hobbies. I want someone who likes the fiction I read, who wants to play D&D with me. I want to be able to talk to someone about my interests and have them be interested too.*

Meanwhile, I wanted someone to create something with. I wanted someone who related to internet culture like me, because for all that I sometimes feel deeply embarrassed about it, it is inescapably *my culture*, all the way back to the early aughts. I wanted someone to argue with for sport. I wanted someone who would say fuck it, let's roll the windows down and sing at the top of our lungs and laugh and talk, the rest can wait, we'll do it later, we'll stay up late and keep laughing and talking while we finish the packing.

What each of us wanted was what the other simply could not provide.

When he mentioned longing for someone to share his hobbies with, I felt a pang of guilt. I had neglected these parts of him, because I sincerely was not interested. They were *his*, things he did alone that I could not bring myself to engage with. He would put on headphones while doing dishes and listen to his favorite podcast, which was a group of people playing D&D. He'd routinely crack up laughing harder than I virtually ever heard him laugh in any other circumstance. I wondered, if I had truly loved him, wouldn't I have naturally expanded my hobbies to include his also? He deserved that.

He connects over his activity-based interests, and I connect over my intellectually-based ones. He primarily *does* and I primarily *think*, and this was our disconnect. My thinking needs took precedence over his doing; he shrank himself to accommodate me. While my romantic passion may have been restrained, and his career may have been the central organizing force of all of our logistics and geography, my personality and interests were center stage, and his faded into the background. We both lost ourselves in this relationship, in different ways. We were safe, but we held each other back.

It dawned on me. He needed the break up as much as I did. I could never, ever love him how he deserved. He would never be able to expand into the fullness of who he is with my force in his life. For all of my guilt about leaving, I now realized, it would be infinitely worse for me to stay. New guilt settled in: I should have done this so much sooner.

**

It has been three hours of staring at my screen. I'm supposed to be packing my apartment to move back to Connecticut permanently. I had moved back to Connecticut in November 2022 with the idea of getting away from California temporarily, being with family and figuring out my own life's direction. I was resisting the inevitable: We needed to break up. Now, it is the third week of January 2023, and we have, and I am surrounded by four-and-a-half years worth of stuff.

Stuff. Stuff is piled around me: clothes, crafting supplies, electronics, puzzles. I need to bring more stuff to the recycling center. Stuff. It's all just stuff. I put the phone down to make lunch and suddenly start shaking with fear. I am afraid of being alone, and so I cry. *What are you doing? Why are you doing this? Are you losing your mind? What if I'm alone forever?* I look down to the ground and fix my gaze on a stain. This is the story I told myself: No one else could possibly love me like he does. No one else could ever love me. I can still hear his words in my head, his arms around me, *Mol, it's never been hard to love you.* Why would I leave this? Foolish and selfish, delusional and ungrateful.

The sky is light blue with streams of thin white clouds crossing paths. I estimate the angles of their overlap at 70 and 110 degrees. I wonder if there have been planes flying recently. My flight is in three days. I have less than 72 hours here. I have spoken to him every single day for eight years and now I won't. I will not see his name, I won't tell him good morning, I won't send him my writing. I won't receive his overflowing encouragement when I feel hopeless.

Why am I doing this? Because I am stuck. Because I have become complacent. I am unhappy. Cared for, adored, but alone. I already feel alone. I have felt alone, completely alone. Now it is laid bare, my loneliness, and it is overwhelming. It spills from my eyes and my pores, it weighs heavy on my chest and chills my skin. I must face it without anyone but my own body and spirit aching for completion.

I come back again to sadness about the weight I must carry alone. I mean this literally: the heaviness of my belongings. My stuff. I mailed 70lb packages of my books and I needed him to carry them into the post office for me. The boxes were too big for my short, clumsy arms to handle. When I go home I will need to bring at least four of these boxes down from the foyer to the basement. He will not be there to do it for me. My atrophy, all of my atrophy, my muscles, my character. The comfort of my self-neglect, the safety of someone else's strength. I must grow now.

I messaged 75 people on Instagram yesterday. I talked to friends for four hours of the day. I argued with strangers, rehearsing my convictions. I had been procrastinating facing the truth, that I am on my own now. This balcony view will never be mine again. This bed I always wished was higher from the ground. The collage I made from our stuff. Our stuff. It's all just stuff. The memories are beautiful but in the past, teeming with ghosts and suffocation. It is time to move on.

**

J, my now ex-boyfriend, brings me to the airport on January 22, 2023. He will drop me off, and that is it. That is the end of our eight years. We stop at the bagel shop for breakfast and I tell him I feel like a timeline has ended.

He says, "Maybe you and I have different ideas of fate, but this is always where we were going to end. We loved each other, we still do, but this is where we were always going to part ways. This is the path you've been on. This was always going to happen."

I know he is right.

Through tears I say, "I don't need to feel ashamed anymore."

"You never had to."

He carries my luggage to the bag drop. We walk to the security line. We embrace each other tightly, with love and grief, as I kiss his chest and he kisses my forehead. We exchange final I love you's and say we know both of us will do great things, that we will both be ok. We set a time to call each other in July to see how life has changed.

We walk away, hands still clasped. His are soft and warm, as they always are, gentle and filled with affection. We make a final moment of eye contact, and with softness, acceptance, let go.

Goodbye, mol.

Goodbye, dof.

Three weeks later

Almost three weeks have passed since my break up. Today is a day I lack faith and focus. I go to the gym for an hour and a half while my mom gets her nails done down the street. I've been lifting weights, something I've wanted to do for years, but never found the courage to follow through on. I haven't had my parents' extra car since before I permanently left California because my brother needs it. I am too broke to buy my own. I work on designing my merch on the treadmill. I finish my workout and use the massage chair. I go home and eat lunch. I practice my harp. I can't complete *Zelda's Lullaby* because my harp does not have enough strings. I figure out the melody of *Go Away and Come Back Hither* and record it, but I don't share it. I do not feel beautiful yet. I have no command over my instrument.

I admit I relapsed and redownloaded Instagram. I had intended to be offline until March. I wanted to show someone how to set up Reels Play bonuses. I zone out for hours on fitness reels and come to, wondering where the day went. I feel like I'm floating. I opened my book draft on my iPad hours ago but cannot bring myself to write. I am emotionally numb, which suggests there is something I am trying to numb from.

I move from my recliner to my bed. My body aches from my exercises. It is 12 degrees today, but I don't know if I could manage much of a walk anyway. I am thinking about protein now. My frozen pasta lunch has 30g. I do math in my head and wish I didn't. It seems unhelpful, a track I don't feel like walking. I don't want to count anything.

Instead, I stare out the window and let the sun into my eyes. It feels soft, like the gentle gaze of someone who loves me. I cry. I miss him. He loved me, and what if no one else will? He saw what is beautiful about me, and what if no one else can? The sun shines brighter into my eyes. In my blindness my chest heaves, a familiar feeling. I don't want to be alone. I text my friend, one of only a few platonic male friends I have. I don't know why, and I don't care to overanalyze it, but in this moment I feel like I need the reassurance of a man.

He quickly replies, "You are incredibly lovable."

It hurts to read, the pain of relief.

I pleaded with God earlier. I asked him to give me strength to push on, to help me concentrate and shift my attention from the immediately gratifying. This year has felt brimming with grace, but today it feels like a big lie, a delusion. I am looking at light shining bright through swaying pine trees and all I can feel is guilt, regret, fear. My cat climbs onto my hip and lays down, looking intently at me. He licks my hand and purrs as I cry.

My loneliness is drowning out my spark, but it is just today. Yesterday I remembered love. Today I doubt I will find it. I know people share my yearnings, because they tell me so when they read my writing. That must mean I will find someone whose yearning unites us together. I cannot know this, I can only have faith.

I couldn't find it in me to make plans to see anyone in California before I left, but I ended up running into my mentor friend. Once I wept on the floor of an office with him, telling him his clarity caused me confusion. I told him I felt gaslit. I wasn't being gaslit, I just felt it, and he was patient and taught me to steady my intellect again. He was never afraid of my intensity; he matched it. He cried too. At the end of our shared geography, I wept next to a cross at the top of a mountain with him. We laughed as we both said "from the cubicle to the crucible."

He and I shared a path and a desire for deep, intimate friendship. I fell in love with him. He did not, which was for the best. I wrote him love letters, but I harnessed my desire into mere friendship. He tells me, "You are trying to reconcile new ideas with old inertia." I have seen too much now and I cannot go back. I wish I could hug him again.

The sunset leaves a pale yellow on the horizon, peeking out from behind those same swaying pine trees. I have stopped crying. I think of words another of my friends has told me throughout our time together: "Go easy on yourself." Her love for me is so pure and I can't believe I found her. I cherish her soft heart. She calls me honey, I call her my love. I admire her strength and beauty. She has tea and toast before bed and sends me photos. When I confess my historical hurts on the phone, she tells me to make myself a snack and be gentle with myself, to take a shower and get to bed early with a cup of tea. I owe her so much. Tonight I will take her advice. I will go easy on myself. I will have toast and tea before bed.

I think of another whose guidance echoed hers: "Just take it easy." He is a foggy parallel and a heartbreaking mirror, and in this I have found the catalysis only painful longing and temptation can prompt. I recall what he said about my sadness. It is the kind that "only someone in the driver's seat of their life feels." I understand this better today. I am driving myself forward, no passenger. Today I fear I've taken a wrong turn, chosen the wrong destination, but that is the risk. I am no longer tagging along or spinning my own wheels. I cannot. I hope it is worth it. I must keep driving, but today is one to pull over and rest. I will take it easy.

One month later

It has been one month since my break up. After eight years coupled, I have now been 30 days single. The first week was hard. Things evened out but often when I leave the gym I feel the urge to cry because I wish I could tell him about it. I know he would be happy for me, proud. I finally started lifting weights like I've wanted to for years. I'm gaining strength more quickly than I anticipated. I celebrate my wins with my best friend. I post them online and people are excited with me. This is when I miss him, or feel remorse.

Why was I never brave enough to pursue my dreams when we were together? In a way it feels like a betrayal, but he never expected anything greater of me than I was at any point. He accepted me in all versions of who I was those eight years, and that was a great, rare gift. I suppose I feel guilt, like I never gave him the best version of me, and I owed it to him. This is part of why I stayed so long. I felt like I was indebted. This is not a reason to stay, nor a reason to improve.

I feel stuck some days. I published my book *Vow*, which I'm excited and nervous to put out in the world, but I look at the length of the life ahead of me and still feel clueless. I feel directionless, lost, or perhaps resigned. I have dreams of road-tripping this summer, of a pilgrimage from France to Spain on the Camino de Santiago, of Ireland. But how? With what money? I don't know yet. For now I spend my days writing, lifting, learning, and talking to a few people here and there.

I feel burnt out on dreaming. Things feel less promising or romantic right now, but I don't mind it. Maybe that was just a stage I needed, a bridge into this next phase. I try to imagine falling in love with someone new and in a way it makes my stomach turn. It feels empty or unsatisfying. I dare anyone to prove me wrong, I guess, but I just don't want it. I can't imagine marriage or children or even what a kiss feels like. It evokes nothing. I flirt on autopilot, as a social instinct, but to what end?

I suppose I am heartbroken. I am also changing. I feel like a hermit. I am not quite struggling but I am maybe digesting. I have tasks left to complete, but I am slow moving. I don't have my own car. I feel forced to stay still, despite my desire to run and adventure. I am trying to obey.

Two months later

I accidentally nap till 11pm then can't fall back asleep. At 3:30am my loneliness is unbearable. At first I don't recognize it for what it is, and then I realize I wish I could roll over into someone's arms. I had gotten into a rhythm this week of messaging a friend past this late hour, but tonight he is not around. I see he has been a crutch, and now I am fully alone, no pacifying distraction. I burst into tears and wail at the empty air, regretting the choice to leave. I have not been touched in two months when I used to be held for hours a day.

I listen to a recording of us talking together to soothe myself, something I have not yet done. I wonder if I should call him. I open his contact card in my phone and stare at the green call button. What would I even say? It's past midnight, why would I bother him? Instead I scroll through photos; I look at our old life. I made the right choice. That isn't what I want anymore. Those aren't my hobbies, my dreams, my language. I am not yearning for what is lost and I cannot pull him into my sorrow. I do not call him. I do not miss him, I am just lonely. We must both move on.

Three months later

I'm having a day where I am so grateful I've made the life choices I've made. I'm happy I am where I am. I am having a lot of realizations about myself, and feel extremely pleased to be an Uncoupled Woman. This morning I woke up well-rested, aching muscles and a hopeful heart. I danced around my kitchen for an hour. I posted a silly little music analysis on my story for fun. I worked out for two hours. These are small things but they are laying groundwork I know I need in order to build something greater in the future. I intended to use this time to recalibrate and it's working.

It has now been three months since my breakup and I am feeling, overall, hopeful and satisfied. There are obviously fears and obstacles on the road ahead. I have my spirals, but I will not be stopped. I am only as paralyzed as I let myself be. Life is a fun story I get to watch unfold before me.

I often wonder how my ex is doing and hope he is well. I'm sure he is and have faith he will do great things. But, I know we both made the right choice to move our lives ahead independently.

It feels good to be alone. It is filled with possibility and potential, two things I love. I've gotten closer to a writer friend, and he has recently encouraged me to apply to law school after I mentioned I was interested but lacked confidence. It has genuinely rejuvenated my optimism. I have no idea if this will lead anywhere but I am so grateful to see a path forward. It is a path that is mine for the taking if I choose it, and I could actually succeed.

I talked to an old friend recently, someone who was absolutely foundational to my life at a pivotal time. We haven't talked since the week of my break up. Our conversation made me realize how much I've changed in this short time. I feel more independent. My entire life is truly different. My visions are crystallizing. I'm not just day-dreaming about a different life, I am literally building it for myself. That is fucking cool.

Break ups are not easy. It hurts to leave someone you love. It is scary to be alone. And then some days, the freedom and possibility are overwhelming in their goodness. I hope you can savor that, the pulsing hope of a new adventure, the creative impulse to write a new story, to meet new people and challenges and expand into a new version of yourself, now alone.

It is a relief to not be constantly weighed down by loneliness. Some days I feel it. I have complex and changing emotions but what I know is that on the whole, I feel joy. I don't mean happy, I mean a kind of faithful ease, deep gratitude. There is a place for me and I will find it.

I recently wrote 4,400 words about falling in love. It was extremely helpful to sort through those ideas, and now that they are out, I feel like I am in a different state of mind. I feel more moti-vated to build my own life and have adventures. Marriage is like a billion years away from where I am right now. I'm content to long when I do, but honestly I'm mostly just enjoying the process of rediscovering myself, expanding my interests, coming back home to the person I always was.

There is no two

In the woods today, I paused to imagine living there. Right there, tucked in trees by the stream. I walked through the mud and felt satisfied with the squish of the earth. The brown stuck on my boot and I admired its richness as the water washed it away. I could fall in love in a forest. I suppose I have, just not with people.

The cottage might be a cabin. If it were a cottage it'd be Irish, made of stone with a red door. If it were a cabin it would be in a New England forest, made of logs. There would be a fireplace and a bookcase built into the wall and a record player and a gas stove and a wired telephone and a big bed with luxurious linens and 19th century art and antique furniture and a window overlooking a vast expanse, and I'd be beautiful in that timeline. I would be enough. I would have found him.

No, I am glad to be alone. Last night I felt the urge to hug a faraway friend, the kind of embrace that melts anguish. The core of me yearned for the comfort of a caring chest to press against. It felt sufficient just to want. I looked beyond that and found I am content to want the blurry outline of whoever I may one day find, if anyone exists who I might be able to call mine. The distance between my heart and some future other is a vista, not a prison yard.

I walked home and recalled the line of a book that felt like fate. It stopped me in my tracks in December. I haven't picked the book back up. It's about an American couple who moved to Ireland to live rurally and write full-time, in the exact place I dream of. The line haunts me. It grounds me into pessimism and hopelessness.

Not everyone can be this lucky. It requires two to have the same shared vision.

Two. I am one, only one. There is no two.

I cannot think in terms of twos. I am content to be one for now, and I must be. The future will turn into the present when the time comes.

It is not a race, but he is winning

It is a late night at the end of May. My heart is aching over various complexities of my life. I open Instagram and look at my personal account, something I rarely do. I hardly ever care what people I went to high school and college with are doing. Babies, traveling, weddings, it does not interest me, they are strangers now anyway.

The first post I see is one of an acquaintance from Santa Cruz. There he is, my ex, sitting in a circle with a group of his friends in a park. My eye is immediately drawn to a girl sitting next to him, a standard personal space distance away. She has curly auburn hair, broad cheeks, fair skin and a long body. She looks, to me, quite plain, but there is an elegance in her limbs. I sense a grounded firmness in her. They are both looking at someone talking in the circle across from them. My body and intuition react before my mind. My stomach drops.

They're in love. He is in love with her.

My heart speeds up with the angst of rejection and competition. It is an impulse to compete not *over* him, but *with* him, a pang of inferiority seeing that he found his before I found mine. Perhaps this is more envy than it is jealousy. I have fallen behind on my goals and my heart feels emptied out over the anguish of an *almost perfect, but...* meanwhile he has found her, a girl who can love him as much as he can love her. I have backslid while he has launched forward. It is not a race, but he is winning, and I am losing, and I am alone, and he is in love.

My rationality catches up with me. They are not even interacting. Not looking at each other, not talking, not touching, They are merely sitting next to each other. Their body language is not directed towards each other, no legs leaning or chest open towards the other. She appears physically closer to the girl next to her than she is to him. There is no, absolutely *no*, indication of intimacy between them. My heart continues beating quickly, now caught in a self-deprecating anxiety about my own strange paranoia, my competitiveness. How on earth could I jump to such an irrational conclusion? And what do I care anyway?

I put down my phone and start to cry. I cannot shake the feeling. *They're in love, and I am utterly alone.*

Yearning

Time to get the apps

My loneliness sinks in concurrent with realizations about what I want. A vision of my ideal love is slowly crystallizing as I am confronted with my increasing hunger to be held. I tell myself my dreaming is mere fiction. I must direct my hands to write rather than my soul to seek. I decide, also, I must root into reality, as bleak as it may be. I must be a single girl in 2023, and if I want any type of intimate connection, I must download An App.

Truthfully, I'm so *bored*. I would like someone to flirt with. I'd love someone to talk to until sunrise, but some playful banter would do. I think I could just go to a bar, but I don't like to drink. I could talk to people at an event, but what kind? And anyway, it's late at night on a weekday. So, I must simply use An App. For no real reason, I download Tinder. I get 600 likes in an hour. Is that a lot? That seems like a lot?

I buy a premium subscription so I can scroll through my digital suitors. Most of them are undesirable, though some are handsome. Every one I talk to, I feel a gap that would be impossible to bridge. I'm not that smart, but these dudes are impressively dull. At the very least, we share no lexicon. These men demonstrate no imagination, no linguistic command. Where is the wit in the wanting?

Neighborhood walk

It is the first bright spring day of the year. I am walking through my childhood neighborhood, enveloped in the visceral promise of new life. The ground is wet from rain yesterday, drying under the warmth of the sun. The scent of grass and asphalt turn into memories of young adventure biking through the forest between streets. I listen to Liquid Smooth by Mitski and feel my body wanting to fulfill its most basic purpose. I recall the rush of new love, the hopeful desire for touch that runs from the back of my neck down to my legs.

A friend's love life makes me believe in God and divine timing. Maybe it will all come together. I lift my face to the sky and bright sun meets my eyes. I close them and I am warm. I remember a first kiss on a log over a river. I remember passion in a secret meadow. It was beautiful to be young. It is beautiful to be who I am now. Lately I've been wondering what my fully embodied sexuality as a 29-year-old woman will look like, shared with another. It isn't that I have been celibate for a decade, but I am now. I am changing and that intimate side of me is too.

I talk about it with a friend. Later that night I talk around it with another. I reflect on it and write and think about the through-line from my youth to now. I suppose I am looking for what is authentic. I want to be authentic in my desires. I want to find the consistent interests and satisfaction and integrate that into something mature. Approaching 30, I'm fully a woman. I feel it now. I sense I have not yet come into a full sense of my sexual self as a woman. Sex is a strange, difficult part of my life to make sense of, and over the last decade, truthfully I tried to avoid fully contending with this. I didn't have pressure to grow.

What do I *want*? Like really and truly *want*? I'm amazed at how I struggle to answer this. There was a time when I was young where this would have been easy, but I was different then. I look different. I'm older. I'm always thinking about and frequently articulating an ideal romantic vision, but what kind of a person would he be? What would actually turn me on? I literally don't know what authentically turns me on anymore.

I swipe through Tinder. No one is particularly captivating. The few people who are end up proving themselves to be dull pretty quickly. I am trying to obey my disgust more, as well as my desire. Someone for whom weed is a personality trait: revulsion. Mid 20s suggesting he's into older women: hot. ENM/poly/open relationship: recoil so fast I don't even blink. This one is interesting to me. Even though I was in an open relationship with J, I found the people I talked to on dating apps who were in their own open setup to be unappealing. Their personalities seem grating, their visages rarely arouse desire in me, and the structured nature of everything seemed inorganic. I like when dynamics emerge naturally, and we make the rules up as we go.

I don't care what people do with their relationships. But I think it's interesting to consider why I find it so undesirable that a potential partner would be non-monogamous, given I was. I don't have interest in involving myself in such a dynamic. I don't feel like vetting the stability of a primary relationship and navigating that. I don't like the cultural baggage it brings, and I don't feel like risking involvement in someone's turbulent relationship. Given my track record of people going inexplicably ballistic at me I would like to minimize my chances of a resentful blow out.

I think about what has the opposite effect of this. The message I got from someone that said "Where do you want to build our cabin?" In response to me saying Ireland: "Are you literally my wife?" This is truly what I want. Not with this random Tinder dude, sorry. I want someone who has a united romantic vision and a desire to commit. I'm not really in the sowing my wild oats era anymore, I don't think, and I'm not really interested in a partner who is either.

I think I do not actually want to be dating. What I want is to excavate the psychology of my romantic and sexual desires in order to ready myself to find love again eventually.

Being received

Last night my best friend said, "I'm so tired of people telling me I'm lovable, that I will have no problem finding someone to love me. If that's true, why hasn't it happened? If I'm so lovable, why has no one loved me?"

I hear her say *lovable* and I think about the support three of my guy friends offered me. One said, "You are incredibly lovable." Another said, "You will absolutely find someone. You will have no trouble finding a man to love you. Plus, you're a girl. You've got that evolutionary advantage." The third said, "You are a very lovable person, intrinsically, as a function of who you are. You deserve love not reactively, but categorically. Many men are going to fall in love with you. The hard part is finding one worthy of you."

Maybe that's my fear, even if it feels self-aggrandizing to put it in those terms myself. Well, I mean, I do fear no one will *want* me in the first place. I don't feel particularly lovable, at least from the perspective of a man. I don't look how I want to and it torments me. I'm not wasting time writing more than that. I'm just unhappy, and my body feels like a prison my beauty will never break out of.

If I can try for a moment to trust that someone could love me, maybe I am afraid I might never be truly in love again. I want to love someone how I loved my first boyfriend as a teen, meaning devoted and passionate, but with the steadiness and security of two grown hearts. And I want it to be someone who is, in my friend's words, *worthy*. But I fear that I won't ever be able to express the expansive, high-energy, devoted, creative and passionate nature of my love.

What would it mean to have someone *worthy*? I wonder what he meant by that. I wonder if he has an idea of what a worthy man would be. When I try to imagine what makes someone worthy, I don't know. Certainly great respect for me, which is matched. Someone who takes me and my potential seriously. Someone who is committed to their own becoming as I am to mine. Someone who is accountable and honest, those are probably the two most critical when it comes to *worthy*. I don't know.

My mind floats back to something that same friend said once, "Knowing you, you are this incredibly passionate, expansive thinker, like that's your whole identity, and to have someone who responds to that by *neutralizing* it? That's unnatural. It's fundamentally wrong." I remember feeling flustered when he said that. I think that's the exact understanding of me that I require, that makes someone *worthy*. I want someone who catalyzes me and challenges me, who I walk with in lockstep towards a shared vision.

Perhaps I am not afraid of not receiving the love I want, but afraid of not finding someone with whom I can fall in love. When I look at the pattern of my recent relational suffering, these weren't actually issues of me not being loved back, per se. More accurately, I would say these were issues of men who could not *receive* me. The three men I became infatuated with over the last few years, they all activated this repressed part of me, my romantic instinct. They were just not ones to give it to. They could not receive it, and in retrospect, none of them are who I want to give it to. I spent eight years with someone who not only could not give me romance, but who did not inspire it in me, and I therefore could not give it. It stayed locked away inside me only to come out when inspired by those unavailable (perhaps, as my friend said: *unworthy*) men.

I am afraid that there is nowhere for me to put all of my love. There is no one who simultaneously inspires it and will want it. I mean really *want* it. Does no one want this who inspires it? Does no one inspire it who is truly worthy of it, in that they are willing to receive it, and return it in their own expression? God, the things I would do for who I am utterly, completely *in love* with. More than I can say, more than I am going to list.

I would write him an entire book. I would send him love letters, even if we lived together I would write them, just because. I would turn our love story into a novel. I would do miserable work to make money for us to afford to live somewhere beautiful. I would cook meat for him! I would suffer to build a life together. I would hold him through tears and guide him softly back to himself. I would run him a bath and kiss his forehead before he leans back and sinks into the water. I would massage him for as long as my hands could manage. I would fly, drive, far and long to be with him, no matter the time or money it would cost. I would ruin lives to defend him. I would be devoted, because I am a devoted person by nature, to that which arouses my devotion, that which I am *in love* with. I am capable of submitting myself to the soul-crushing daily slog, and would do it especially for someone I am *in love* with. I would be so attentive I would memorize everything about him without effort, just because I feel a passion that is innate, immutable, always present.

Will anyone want this from me who I want to give it to? Will anyone want to spend their life by my side, laughing, talking, dreaming, adventuring and creating something beyond my individual imagination? I don't know how I'll ever find this. I imagine it takes a mixture of prayer and "putting myself out there." Where is "out there"? Maybe traveling. Possibly school. Definitely not bars. Probably not Instagram. That hasn't proven very fruitful.

I've never been courted. I want someone to set their sights on me and draw me in. But I wonder if I could actually stand being in that position, given my pathological need to be in the driver's seat of romance. It just would be nice to not have to be the relational mastermind for *once* in my *stupid* life. I am always the cat, never the mouse; always the seeker, never the treasure. I may never find the love I've yearned for, and so be it. I literally cannot predict the future. I can just work on clarifying my ideas and desires, and ready myself to be worthy of a man worthy of me also. I hope he's out there. Probably I ought to just write some novels and move on.

Can love be cutting?

When I was 18 I was in a chaotic, destructive relationship. Once it finally was over I became terrified of myself and my own intensity. I developed beliefs about myself, love, and relationships that were rooted in irrational fear of myself. I thought I was, at my core, dangerous or crazy. I took a vow not to love again.

One of our dynamics was me calling him on ways he was manipulative and dishonest. I look back now and see I was, ultimately, trying to hold him accountable to what I knew he aspired to be and I believed he was capable of becoming. I saw through his defenses and grandiosity and called him on this. I was deeply invested in his integrity.

At the time, my choice to challenge him did not go over well. He could not handle the blows to his ego. If he could, he wouldn't need all the defenses. I was not helpful, I was harsh, nor was I omniscient and sometimes missed the mark. I could not withstand either his reactive lashing out or his self-flagellation. Neither of us were mature or steady enough for such a dynamic. We ended up treating each other poorly. We were, of course, kids. It happens.

Now, ten years later, this guy and I are friends. We are on good terms and look back at our history with an appreciation for the absurd. He has recognized shortcomings through the years that are indeed related to the ones I tried, ungracefully, to point out in our youth.

Reflecting on this laid bare something I've been building up to for over a year: I'm actually not fucking crazy. I don't need to be afraid of my passion. I was onto something back then, and even was correct in much of my analysis. My problem wasn't that I was being Bad, it's that I was a teenager dating another teenager and neither of us were ready for love. We were both traumatized and struggling, trying to repair ourselves and each other but unable to. I realize what I was trying to give him *was* actually love. I was clumsy and cutting, he was an exposed nerve. The vow I took to never feel passion again was misguided. I was afraid of myself, but I do not have to be.

My impulse to cut through deceit and confront the person I love with a mirror to the ways they are falling short of their own integrity is actually, to those who want and can receive it, an act of immense love. Done skillfully, this is part of willing the good of another. Coming to accept and love this about myself, moving it out of shame, this has been part of my journey to womanhood. I see this now as a feature of femininity, and I love it. It is necessary, not bad, just a skill to build so it becomes an instrument of love rather than a weapon for cruelty.

I wonder if I could find a man who wants this. I think I could love like this again, better this time, gentler, less selfishly.

God am I just sapiosexual?

What if I could commit to someone? I wonder this a lot, and then I realize: I obviously *can*. What do you call eight years of a relationship? The better question, then, is: What if I could commit to someone and *want to*? And I don't mean I want to stay because it is safe and familiar, like I did in this last relationship. I mean I want to stay because it is satisfying at such a deep, libidinal level that I never want to let it go. Of course the other order compatibilities would be there, but what if I could find something so *primally* satisfying, it makes the drudgeries, our conflicts, all worth the effort?

Could I ever find a relationship that feels like a lifelong supply of mental stimulation? That is erotic to me, or at least I think it must be a precondition to accessing the full potential of the erotic. Satisfying the cerebral is a gateway to satisfying the primal. I wonder if this is possible, if there is someone whose mind I might never tire of, whose rhythms spark desire in me even as they grow familiar.

That's how it works with me, it's primarily about the mind. I don't think I care so much if their body breaks down, if it changes and expands or shrinks or what have you. I suppose I need the pheromones to hit right, and to be enamored of how their body moves through space, but this is the animation of the spirit through the body anyway. If their soul's expression through movement is what I love, then their physique is secondary. I might love it in all forms. But first of all: I want their brilliance.

The body, rather than being the first site of desire, is a site for expression of a preexisting libidinal flow between intellects. I wonder if acting on this would make sex truly pleasurable to me, if my imagination could collide with someone else's before our bodies do. I live in the world of narrative fantasy. Everything is a story unfolding always. Why else would I write so much about my own life? I think in terms of arcs, twists, and subtext. If I could find someone who lives in fantasy also, and if our fantasy worlds might overlap, might I finally be able to feel what I hoped sex could be?

What if I could find someone with whom our entire dynamic is a state of constant foreplay, psychological stimulation that organically makes way for consummation through the sexual? If I am not only completely enthralled with someone's intellect, but in an active dynamic with an effortless reciprocal flow, I imagine sex could be the ultimate meeting of minds: nerves colliding through skin, the ecstatic exchange of electricity at one's most sensitive points of conduction.

Why does this seem to come so easily to everyone else? I make it all too complicated. I wish I could think less, or just have no drive for union whatsoever, but I do. But then I wonder: What if the issue isn't that I think too much, but that I need someone who thinks like me?

I started writing letters to my future husband in April

My love one day I will be warm for you again. I will not let this freeze me. I promise I will find you.

**

I want to watch the sunset with you and listen to the night sounds of summer fade in alongside twilight. I wonder if we'll ever have the cottage, maybe the cabin too, or just one or the other, or maybe we'll find a new dream together. I can't wait to smile at how much bigger your hands are than mine.

**

I would spend a life loyal to our vision of greatness. Each of my nerves reaches for you, only for you, who I have been seeking all my days.

**

I have been moved to write by yearning for others, but that

writing is the fruit of a different tree. I write to you tonight from the most secret part of me, which is not the frenzied one I banished in shame of my own wanting. I write to you from the indestructible essence of me, the core that has survived despite the varied wars of being human, even as its dominance is tested in battle; the part of me that knows beyond a shadow of a doubt I am here for a purpose greater than the force of anyone else's violence, of my self-sustained exile or doubt. I write to you from my most holy conviction: God created me to love you. I have always loved you, and I always will.

**

Maybe our storylines won't collide until we have aged, once we are wizened and weary. I will love you through a broken hip or a heart attack. I will sit by your side and read you your favorite book as you weave between life and death. I will light candles and play your favorite music as you take your last breath. For every day of mine that remains, I will write to you even still.

Evolutionarily sub-optimal

Being newly single, I am far more self-conscious of my potential desirability and undesirability. At times, this self-awareness is literally the most paralyzing force I have encountered since the various existential crises in my 20s about the limiting force of social conditions and my powerlessness to change them. Looking in the mirror hurts about as much as contending with capitalist realism lately.

I am confident in so many ways: speaking my mind, making requests, intervening, writing, other things. I don't actually value my appearance that highly on my own, but I feel excruciatingly aware that it is such a limiting factor in other people valuing me. I feel like I understand incels right now. Like, the amount of neurotic self-loathing and fear of rejection I have about the gap between what I see as my reality and everyone else's ideal is crazy.

Something that is inescapable about my mind is that it always returns to evolutionary basics. I feel acutely aware of the nature of male attraction being so visual, and the sense that I am visually sub-optimal to a high degree, and how that will limit my chance at love. I'm struggling with what of that is simply realism and what of it is actually a black-and-white cognitive distortion.

What if this stupid physical form, this thing I wish I could simply transcend into being pure mind or spirit, will forever be my biggest obstacle? What if this flesh, the very means through which two minds can actually merge, becomes the very barrier to my ability to do just that?

What if I meet someone otherwise perfectly aligned with me, but my weight, this stupid battle with appetite and hedonism, renders me unavoidably unattractive at a basic biological level? Then that's that, I guess. There's the whisper of "Well they just aren't the one for you!" I can't buy that shit. It's just so frustrating.

I wish I didn't have to think like this. So I try to remind myself of what I know to be true, given my own experience of attraction: It is simply not reducible to one dimension. I literally am attracted to so many women, including women who look like me. I am not necessarily attracted to a particular physique, I am attracted to how the body is animated by the spirit and mind.

The way someone moves through space is what spellbinds me in terms of physical attraction, maybe especially with men. I fall in love with mannerisms, walks, facial expressions, the way someone looks at me, the way they smell, so much more than features or size or whatever else.

This is comforting for moments until I return to biological basics, and I spiral again. Perhaps the issue is deeper, like this is an expression of an inescapable narcissism inherent to my psychology that makes feeling "low status" especially paralyzing. How boring. Be mid, happy and free you nerd.

I feel acutely aware of hierarchical social organizing while also genuinely wanting to, mostly, reject or transcend it. But I don't think that is realistic. But I want to strive for it because I'm an idealist and believe everyone has inherent value and I have a moral conviction against hierarchical oppression. But this is humanity and not Heaven, so I must remain cripplingly self-aware of my inferiority on Earth and pray I find someone else who thinks like me and I guess wants to bang like once a month.

Honestly though my perfect mate would absolutely share my

experience of attraction because I would basically share a brain with that person which would be 500x more erotic than physique and since our brains would be so in sync they'd feel the same and then we'd float away into non corporeal space, how can I find this on a dating app?

Anyway all I can do when I hate myself is take small steps towards improving my self-image so that's what I do. Moisturize, perfume, nice dresses, blow dry my hair, makeup, lift weights, whatever. It helps a little. One day I'll be super old and none of this dumb shit will be relevant.

The state of being in love

Last night my friend expressed a common cynical sentiment about love, one I always roll my eyes at. The experience of being "in love" is "rare and random and physiochemical." It is an unpredictable, *fleeting* emotion. He is correct that it is *rare*, but I do not believe it is *random*, though it is unpredictable. To be *in love* is to feel a bond that defies reason but awakens an unmatched tenderness, selfless devotion, a desire to nurture and protect, a glow of admiration for their inner and outer beauty, and motivation to become greater in order to maximize the strength of the bond between you and the other. It is not merely a feeling, but it is something that is primarily recognized through feeling. It emerges in our awareness through physiochemical processes that evoke *feelings*, ok, but that alone is not the bond, that is the expression of the bond. I think that bond between two people is something that has always been, even before their meeting. It is a fundamental state of being between two people.

In this, there is an essence that is unavoidably romantic, by which I mean, maybe, a spark of energy between two that could under the right circumstances create something great: maybe an actual baby, maybe an empire. I think to be truly *in love* is necessarily mutual. If it's unrequited it is perhaps not love but admiration, though it's easier and more culturally legible to say "I fell in love but he didn't love me back." But in my little conceptual world it's different.

To be *in love* is not simply a fantasyland. It is rooted in the most basic part of being alive: to reproduce. It is fundamental reality, elevated, intensified. It is a deep desire for union and transformation in large part born of the potential to create and maximize conditions for what is created to thrive. I see reproduction as spiritual; it is the act of creation, the most direct reflection of what first created us.

The energetic tie between two people in love is something spiritual, and this is why I say it is not random, and that it has always *been*. We feel it as random because we cannot predict it until it has already passed some sensory threshold, so it seemingly emerges from nowhere, patternless in our measurement, but it is part of a pattern beyond mere physical attraction. It's an event in a metaphysical storyline progression; it is a story God writes that we cannot fully predict. Our choice comes in what we do with the bond, if we nurture or abandon it. This is the tragedy of fate: it comes with free will, and often people make catastrophic errors in judgment.

Perhaps my idea of being in love as an extension of reproductive possibility is why I cannot imagine myself truly falling in love with a woman, despite my suspicion that the intensity of my romance is so inevitably feminine and would be best matched in its expression by sapphic love. But conceptually, spiritually I think it is fundamentally tied up in reproduction for me, which is obviously heterosexual. I can't imagine being *in love with* another woman. Maybe this is a problem of the limitations of my fantasy, but I can't decide if the issue is in my sexual fantasy of women or my romantic fantasy of men. I've simply never felt romantic desire for a woman, though I am primarily erotically attracted to them.

Maybe this also reveals how I differentiate romantic love from the love between mere friends. I do not want to build a life *with* a female friend with whom I share dreams, have a matched conversational intensity, a mutual commitment to our connection, and for whom I have a deep appreciation of her beauty. The depth of our friendship makes it such that I do not want to have sex with her. This is the opposite of my experience with men, I think. I do not wish I could *create* with her, in a primal sense, and I wonder if it is because we cannot. Probably I'm constraining my imagination, but I guess the truth of the matter is, I've never fallen in love with a woman, and I can't see myself doing it in the future, but I'm open to anything.

This reminds me of what I wrote about romance years ago: *Romance is growth alongside each other, not just bearing witness from the sidelines.* One of my closest friends and I are on parallel paths in uncanny ways, and we do carry each other through it. But I suppose it feels different from being *alongside.* The way she and I are alongside each other is like holding hands across dimensions and steadying each other along rocky points in our respective paths. The way I imagine *alongside* in a romantic context means you are sharing the same path.

Yet, sometimes I think I might not find love with a man. I'm sort of instinctively emasculating, if only by virtue of my self-expression. Maybe I just need to embrace my inner dominatrix. I think I just need to find a guy who's into that but still is a dominant force independently. I suspect I will never in my life be someone who can reign in my instinct to snap or scold when I feel my autonomy or self-authority is being undermined. It's my communication style and I...like it. I like being forceful and firm when the situation calls for it. I like friction! I like power! It's my Enneagram eight wing. Obviously I can HR-ify my communication but I don't want to have to always be gentle with my life partner, how insufferable and confining. I'm not gentle! I can be, but I'm by nature quite sharp and extremely resistant to authority or control being exerted over me, especially by men.

Once my ex said I am a "high octane experience that requires thick skin and the ability to roll with the punches." This actively turned me on. Is it bad that I like that about myself? I don't want something effortless. I don't want love to always be easy, lazy, or comfortable. How boring. It sounds understimulating. I want someone I could fight with. I want to argue for sport and sex. But I *need* someone who will ultimately defer to my authority over the matters in which I truly have authority, like *myself*. Or knowing which way to go when driving. I'm so annoying. But also this would probably be extremely hot for someone? Maybe? Do these men exist?

Another major piece for me is the drive to know. The state of being *in love* drives me to know someone in full. There is the curiosity I feel with all people, of course. I love knowing people, but I don't want to *excavate* everyone. That is born of the process of falling in love. It is a feedback loop in that the deeper I excavate the deeper I fall, maybe a bit like tunneling into discovering a beautiful cave. Best metaphor yet. I need to go to New Mexico. Of course then sometimes I begin excavation and realize it's a dead end, then move on. Usually this doesn't take too long.

I think of one man I became infatuated with, who did not reciprocate my feelings. I developed theories of him. I studied him, deep dives in my writing and my thoughts. To my knowledge no one has treated me this way. No one has tried excavating me like I have them. I wonder what it might be like to find a person who shares this intensity in pursuit of romance. I wish I could be the object of a person's tunnel vision. I want eyes boring into mine. I want an essay, a song, art. Not mere admiration: mutual desire, matched skill.

The aphorism *Love is a choice* is an incomplete definition. My entire relationship was about *choice*. I chose him intentionally, I chose to love him, I chose to stay, but it did not start from a place of passion. And *that* is the problem. The foundation of the choice must be rooted in the experience of falling *passionately* in love. If I fall in love, and if I am to create, I want what is created to emerge from a great explosion, not the energetic equivalent of selecting a job candidate.

Love is not only a verb. Love is not only a choice. What a sad, pathetic, sanitized vision of the most intimate human relationship, stripped of the profound spiritual experience of deep and abiding romantic love. It's the worst type of Instagram therapy nihilism, turning *love* into yet another obligation, another mere drudgery, like a desk job you settle into to pay the bills. I don't want Protestant work ethic love. I want Catholic high drama love, you boring, unimaginative, passionless freaks.

I don't want a rock

I never again want to describe my partner as my *rock* or my *anchor*. I don't want to be with someone whose primary function in my life is to care for or protect me, because we are two full grown adults. That is not a partnership, that is a caregiving dynamic. The unfortunate reality of my relationship is that at many points, that is what it became: I was unwell, and he nurtured me. I am sure we have both come to regret this. I always have.

A friend of mine once said he believes all modern romantic relationships are basically just a race to be the child instead of the parent. I do not want to participate in such a race, if that's true. I want something fiercely complementary and reciprocal. It is not a practice in making up for shitty parenting or outsourcing emotional regulation. Those things happen, but they are secondary.

The cornerstone of enduring romantic love is sharing the unadulterated essence of you and having it met with adoration and complementarity. If you are constantly responsible for each other's emotional stability, you cannot fully be yourself, because the role you perform for the other takes primacy over authentic self-expression. If you cannot be your true selves together, deep intimacy cannot be achieved. In love, both people ought to have full, free reign to express their truest selves, unmasked and unashamed, met with affection.

The *rock* of the relationship is not the emotional sturdiness of one or the other, it's a shared commitment to a higher purpose. I envision a relationship that serves a higher goal. It is generative and productive. Something is created from it, and to serve that purpose, each person has a responsibility to themselves and each other to optimize conditions for a stable, satisfying, flowing dynamic. We stabilize ourselves and each other in order to move towards the shared vision. We love each other and want each other to flourish as individuals, and we grow reaching up towards that great hope we both share.

Obviously being in love inspires you to care for each other, which is literally the foundation of human bonding. But there is a line between mutual support and unbalanced giving. There are times when care may be inequitable, especially in advanced age, but possibly sooner if one becomes sick. Caring for one another is part of the commitment you make to combining lives. *In sickness and in health* and so on. But when nurturing someone is the primary function? No thanks. I do not want to be on either side of that equation. I'll have a baby if I want to do that. Or I'll call my mom, or get a therapist or something.

The ideal love is not one of being merely cared for or tended to for the purpose of being pacified at worst, healed at best. I do not seek a parent or a project or a redeemer in a lover. I am not my lover's child, they are not mine. I am their collaborator. I am not a wound for them to tend, nor a womb for them to grow in. I am a partner in creation.

I want to claim and be claimed

I think I want to feel jealous again. I used to pride myself on *not being a jealous person*. I thought there was virtue in transcending jealousy, either that *I* was secure, or my *relationship* was secure. I see now that actually, my lack of jealousy was a symptom of a lack of deep romantic love. It was a sign not of security, but indifference.

What would it feel like to want someone enough to be truly jealous? I want to love and *crave* someone so much I fear losing their affection. I want someone who fears losing my affection too. I do want that, and I'm tired of pretending I don't. I'm uninterested in the idea of neutralizing jealousy. No, jealousy is a *good* thing; it is a demonstration of genuine attachment and a belief in the value of the other person.

Yes, it is also obviously born of insecurity. Some people are excessively jealous because they are excessively insecure, or overly dependent. But like, come on. Let me have this. A little jealousy would feel great, you know? In what world did I think I'd ever be satisfied with mere indifference?

I want to claim and be claimed. I say this and think about the lyrics to a song I used to listen to a lot when I was 19, a decade ago, in the midst of an early bout of mental upheaval. At that point in my life, I was in a new, strange type of pain. I was psychically un-moored, dissociated and panicking virtually all the time. I managed to hold it together academically, but socially and internally I was barely functional. Spiritually, I felt dead, possessed by an existential hopelessness that left me unconsciously wondering if I had entered hell. The song is *The Nothing Part II* by Lady Lamb.

Lay me down, Lay me low
Let go your crown, Disarm me
Singing
Take me south, Take me home
Hold your own, and claim me

The lyrics themselves were not necessarily as powerful to me as the sound of the sweeping chorus that sang them. But the words *claim me* always stick out. Yes, I want that. The open relationship situation I had with my ex was, in my opinion, in retrospect, a disaster from every angle. It was a loose agreement we had from the beginning of the relationship. But it was symptomatic of the core incompatibility, a sign of the inevitably unsatisfying chemistry be-tween us. Neither of us really *wanted* each other that much. We did not feel moved to fully claim the other.

I used to put that song on at work after the shop closed and it was time to clean. I'd blast it and throw my head back in a kind of musical ecstasy at these lyrics. It was a rare reprieve from my suffer-ing. I want a love that feels like this song felt to me back then: like relief, like hope, like surrender, like home, like it's all worth fucking fighting for.

Advising

When safe is not enough

You told yourself you'll never fall in love again like you did that first time, when the object of your passionate devotion tore your heart out, crushed your spirit, made you believe you aren't built for love. You scared yourself in the enormity of your own desire and fear, and you swore you'd never let anyone, not even yourself, touch that part of you again.

You take a vow to never love again. But then you are lonely, and you are yearning, but you must stay resolute. It feels like sobriety: When I am in love I am a monster, and so I will not let myself touch such passion. One day a patient soul teaches you it is safe to be held. You cry on the phone, you sob into their chest, they tell you it is safe and they are right. It is safe. They love you, they are beautiful, and you feel sober. You are not crazy. Their words are not weapons, but a balm and a warm embrace.

Then, one day, perhaps gradually, perhaps all at once, you realize you are deeply unsatisfied. A slow awareness builds: This is not *enough*. What happens when you have committed to what is safe, but you still yearn to feel that passionate love, that ambitious hope, that overflow of romance your heart once felt before the first arresting wound? What happens when you start to doubt that this safe, beautiful person is someone you can really, truly, choose? You chose them because the love was sturdy, gentle, yet that romantic desire cannot be satisfied. You try, but this person, their generosity and devotion—why is it not enough for you? Why are you so restless?

Perhaps it is dispositional. You have the person so many would love to have, but you are not satisfied. This must be a you problem. What do you do with the guilt, the self-loathing, the newest reason to believe you are somehow wrong, too monstrous, too selfish? Passionate love is not for you, nor is patient love, it seems, so what will you do?

You stay. In a way, you feel indebted. They loved you through the wounds, they taught you how to receive love again. You learned it is safe to be loved. You softened to them, and you returned their affection. But what about that passion? Maybe you are not restless, dispositionally impaired. Maybe you committed to a relationship that is, at its core, not passionate, not reciprocal in its devotion. Maybe, painfully, you are not wholly in love.

It is here, in the admission, that you have another chance to stay or go. You stay, again. You must at least give them two more good years, until some milestone. You must keep trying. You must stop believing in fairytales and myths about romance. This is a healthy, stable love. It is enough. But that hunger never quiets, and then one day, you meet someone who makes the craving unbearable. The house of cards falls apart, the resentments cascade, the logic of fear crumbles beneath the power of desire.

You can choose again to stay or go. This is the breaking point. This was my breaking point. I had a brief encounter with someone who unleashed a vision and a burning desire that eventually made me realize I would never, ever be able to commit to building a life with the safe, devoted partner I had been so blessed to be with. I was not being honest with myself, and I was wronging him by choosing him from a place of fear and guilt. I needed to leave, not to be with that other person—they were evidently uninterested and a total mismatch—but because through them I had been confronted with truth.

Breaking up with someone who is frankly a lovely person, but is ultimately incompatible with you, is extremely difficult. It is a hard decision to make because it seems irrational. But love is not a fully rational experience. Falling deeply in love is not always dangerous, but it will not always feel completely safe because intimacy involves both pleasure *and* pain, especially for the sensitive romantics among us. If you are prioritizing safety, choosing someone out of habit while yearning for more, you are in a relationship out of self-preservation. That is fair to neither of you. It is ok to leave.

Not everyone shares this conviction, I know, and it probably sounds delusional to many. But, in the core of me I believe that, if I am meant for the partnership I have always desired for as long as I can remember, then I will find it when I am ready. I believe that person, if they do exist, is readying themselves also. I feel it in my soul, and I have faith that if God wills it (not only if I desire it), then it will happen—but only if I have created space in my life for a partnership. So I am single, and I am working on myself, and my hope wavers, but I give it to God.

Biological clock

It is tempting to deny the need to break up with someone, simply because you fear your biological clock. Especially if the relationship is fairly stable. It seems like fair-ish strategy at first glance: Why leave stable, "enough," when you're running out of time to have kids? Why try finding better love, why not settle?

This sucks about being a woman, genuinely. I get it. I'm 29 right now, and I am all too aware that I'm running out of time to have kids in a way I barely had to consider when I was even just like, 25. Aging played a role in talking myself out of the idea of leaving. The prospect of having to find someone new to settle down with is terrifying. The reality is there are a lot of shitty people out there, it's true.

But also: Do you actually *want* to have kids with the person you're with? I look at people who have kids in my life and it looks brutal. It pushes people to the edge. It stretches even great relationships thin. I came to realize I simply could not raise kids with my ex. Through the years, as I expanded into my own person—for example, exploring religion—it became increasingly apparent that we would run into a lot of conflict with child-rearing.

Also consider if you'd like their family involved in your child-rearing. If you already have doubts about the relationship itself, what if you don't really like their family? Obviously every situation is different, but that could become yet another site of conflict and incompatibility: your partner's family's involvement in childrearing.

I know that the tick-tock of your biological clock is nerve wracking, but also...if you doubt your relationship right now, what do you think would change when it comes to having kids? In my case, I decided that the doubts would intensify, the stress would increase, and it would make raising kids *extra* challenging. A significant part of my justification for staying with my ex was *he would be such a great father.* I still believe that; he will be an amazing father for *sure.* But would we make a good parenting duo? No.

The other thing is: How much do you actually want kids anyway? This is something I still don't have an answer to. I was procrastinating ending a relationship situation because of a potential future that I'm not even sure I care that much about anyway. I don't know if I could be a mother for a lot of reasons. What I have heard people say throughout my life is *You know you'll want kids when you find the person you want to have them with.* So far I have not found that person, and it definitely was not my ex. The point is, I strongly encourage you to make decisions based on what you *know* you want— need!—rather than a fear about an obstacle to a future that you are ambivalent about.

On the other hand, there are many times when I wish I did it sooner precisely because of my clock.

When I was 25, I finally saw a psychiatrist. My mental health had reached a breaking point for myriad reasons, and therapy and self-help simply could not cut it. I got on the right medication and I felt like myself for the first time in a decade. I had not felt so present and emotionally stable since I was 15 years old.

My ex and I shared a birthday. Three of the four birthdays between meeting that man and breaking up with my ex, I was mentally preoccupied with other things, and I felt a simmering frustration with my relationship. I tried to push it out of my mind, tell myself the same story: *I am restless, I am ungrateful.* Back and forth between *This isn't enough* and *This is more than you deserve.* I wish I had believed myself. I wish I had the courage to end things. I wish I did it sooner.

By 25, I could tell I wanted out. It was obvious, but my gymnastics were too powerful a defense from truth. I knew I wanted a creative partnership. I knew I wanted a relationship that was not just about comfort, but higher purpose. I'm 29 now and I sincerely wish I had an older woman in my life who sat me down and gave me this frank advice:

If you know, and it sounds like you *know*, that this man is not who you *want* to spend your entire life with, then you need to leave him. This will keep happening. You will keep finding new situations to escape into, and it's not because you are doomed to be this way; it is because you are unsatisfied. You will never find *perfect*, but you can find someone who *satisfies* you enough to make the boring slog worth it.

You are 25 years old right now. The reality is that you are a woman, not a man, and that comes with built-in restrictions. You are a woman who is getting older, and if you know that he is not the one you want to commit to, and you think you so much as *might* want to have kids one day, you need to take your biological limitations seriously. You are a woman. You will not be able to get pregnant after a certain point.

I know, you don't want kids *right now*, but what do you expect to happen when you finally realize you *do* want them? You need to think strategically about this, and you need to think long-term. It takes time to find someone to settle down with. It takes effort: dating, vetting, then marrying, and then conceiving, and then birthing. That whole process can take years.

You are 25 years old right now, and you do not have a career built for yourself yet. You do not have a career, nor a partner who you can see yourself committing to. You need to leave him. You need to figure out what you want to do with yourself, on your own, what your dreams are, and then you will find someone when the time comes. He will recover and build a life of his own. You are not indebted to him. You will recover and build a life of your own. You are not unlovable.

You deserve something satisfying, and so does he. When you leave, he will tend to himself, and he has people who will help him. And so do *you*. You are still young, but you will not always be, and the longer you wait, coasting, spinning your wheels as he builds a career and you flounder in dead-end jobs just to pay rent, the harder everything is going to be.

Do not make your future that much harder on yourself just because you feel guilty that you were sick. Do not sabotage yourself because of fear. You are not bad. You can end things, and you will be grateful you did, even in the pain, especially after it.

You are allowed to leave

I see so much writing about what it's like to be someone who your partner (usually a man) is refusing to fully commit to. If someone cannot choose you, leave. If he wanted to, he would. Many words of comfort and guidance are offered to those who are not being chosen, which generally amount to: Develop enough self-worth to leave and find someone who will choose you. You deserve unambiguous commitment.

I agree with this, but what if you are the one who can't choose someone, can't commit? You want to love your partner, you tell yourself you do, and you see how much they deserve love—but what if you cannot be the one who gives it? What if you love someone but you are, simply, not *in love*?

A major impediment to me leaving was feeling like a raging narcissist. How could I possibly justify leaving someone who, in my view, sacrificed so much of his time and energy to love me, who was devoted and ever-patient? How could I abandon him, leaving him to pay absurdly high rent, or be forced to live with (*shudder*) room-mates? I felt I owed him a type of care I feared I never could reciprocate. This was never his view, but it was part of my choice to stay.

And what kind of selfish moron leaves someone to pursue a fantasy? Who am I to say that such a beautiful person *isn't enough* to satisfy my fanciful romantic daydreams? I don't like to restrict my imagination to a dichotomy of hero or villain, but it made me truly feel villainous, the idea of leaving someone who had given me so much, in pursuit of some Great Hope. He taught me it was safe to love again. He gave me eight years of his young life, putting up with me when I was sick, failing, flailing. And he loved me, generously, unconditionally. What the hell else could I want? Why could I not just give this back to him? Why could I not give him a lifetime? He didn't ask for that; we agreed we weren't ready for marriage. But I tormented myself about it nonetheless.

My best friend got divorced this year. The process started last year. Our situations are not perfect parallels, but there is some overlap, and we were in reversed roles. Her ex was in my role in terms of not being fully satisfied. My ex was in my best friend's role of being satisfied to fully commit. It manifested differently in our relationships, the details of which are irrelevant. The point is, she had insight into the other side, albeit in a much more extreme version.

She urged me to leave. She said she wished her ex had found the courage to leave, but instead she suffered through trying to be enough, and had to then be the one to end it. She resented, and was hurt by, her ex's complete inability to take responsibility for his true desires. Instead, she suffered under their weight throughout the relationship, and then finally had to be the one to lift it and end the relationship. She urged me to take responsibility for myself. I saw her point.

I told her I felt riddled with guilt, and I still do after the fact, and she tells me, "You only need to feel guilty if you stay. You left. You did the right thing, and he will be fine."

I think about this a lot. It is correct to feel guilt if you stay, knowing that you want more, unable to truly give yourself to your partner. That guilt ought to be fuel for action. If you stay, knowingly deceiving them, for whatever reason, it is reason for guilt, which ought to urge you to leave.

I talked to a friend recently about my break up, and he commented that it was *bold* to leave in pursuit of a *grandiose yearning*. I know, and judging that as bad or selfish is part of what kept me around so long. I first felt a strong sense that I really wanted a different type of relationship back in late 2019. It took me over three years and a major spiritual conversion to finally pull the trigger. This is not an easy process. It is ok if it is slow. It makes sense to be thorough, but eventually you *need* to make the call.

If you have had years of doubt, it might be worth considering if you are overintellectualizing, holding too firmly onto a "rational" calculus at the expense of genuinely considering your emotions. Feelings matter as much as reason. I refused to let my feelings guide me. I always found ways to justify or rationalize or minimize. I effectively was gaslighting myself. I was dismissing my feelings and straight up pathologizing them.

Like, no, it's not actually narcissistic to realize you have become so comfortable in a stable relationship that you've lost your own path, and need to become independent again; to want a deep romantic love or a creative partnership that is simply not now or ever what your current partner will provide; to leave someone when your visions for the future are not in alignment, even if they are a wonderful person.

If they are a wonderful person, then let them go so they can find someone else wonderful who is aligned with their vision. You don't need to compromise yours, they don't need to compromise theirs, and you aren't bad. You do not need to torture yourself with guilt and shame.

I believed I was indebted to him at certain points. I remember questioning the relationship in early 2019, crying on the phone with my best friend, and I told her *I feel like I owe him at least three more good years.* She told me that was a ridiculous reason to stay with someone, that relationships are not so transactional. I obviously *knew* that and would tell anyone else the same thing. But I really don't know how to express the depth of guilt I felt, knowing that this man was steadfast throughout my years of active mental illness —and now that I'm well, I have the audacity to consider *leaving*? (I did not actually consciously stay with him for three more years, trying to "make it up" to him, but it turns out that we ended up staying together that much longer.)

That is not reasonable. You are not held hostage to someone's love and kindness. You are not obligated to stay in a romantic relationship, even with someone who gave you a tremendous amount of selfless love during turbulent times. It's ok to leave a relationship with someone who supported you deeply. You are *not* bound to them by a cosmic debt. You have the freedom to leave. Guilt is not the right foundation for a relationship, and you can try convincing yourself that the guilt is love—but eventually you need to be honest with yourself.

In fact, if a romantic relationship—in my opinion, especially one that has not been vowed to marriage—is primarily a dynamic of caregiving, it is not one to stay in. That is not a romantic dynamic at all, really. If the dynamic has become something like parent/child, this is not a life partnership. It is a developmentally arresting circumstance. Obviously there will always be a level of mutual caregiving, and at certain times it is likely going to be that one needs more than the other, but if a parent/child flow is at the foundation of your dynamic, that is unsustainable, and unfair to both of you.

Also keep in mind that you can still love and support your partner, offer them care, but in a way that is not in the context of a romantic relationship. The transition into friendship may take time, but it's possible. And sometimes, leaving someone's life is actually a great gift—not because you were a "toxic" influence, just because loss is often a catalyst that forces us to grow. Losing what we once depended on forces us to become more fully ourselves. You have no idea how it will change their life. All you can do is be honest and compassionate with how you end it.

The flip side, of course, is the people who have taken on a role of caregiver in their romantic relationship, but feel like they want to end it. This is another heavy feeling of guilt in the form of feeling that you are abandoning your partner. One of my strongest convictions, one that is not always easy for me to accept, but is true and necessary to become an adult: in an adult relationship, a break up is not abandonment. It is a painful life experience, obviously. It will cause an increase in stress. But that is, unfortunately, just life. Life is painful. Staying with someone you want to leave is painful. Putting your life on hold and prioritizing the needs of someone you no longer want to be tied to is painful. It's all painful, but decisions made from honesty are the best balm. Truth and time will heal the wound.

Adult romantic relationships are not like parent/child relationships; you cannot truly abandon your romantic partner, because they are not dependent on you for survival. Adults are responsible for taking care of themselves, building a support network and finding resources to take care of themselves. It is not abandonment to end a romantic relationship, even if it feels deeply painful. Also remember ending a romantic or sexual dynamic does not mean that you need to leave someone's life completely and forever.

Another struggle with deciding to leave is *timing*. It's just not the *right time* to break up. *I need to give him three more good years.* In some ways, I do believe that there is a kind of divine timing to everything, but we've also got to take action. But, even when the signs are there, when it is staring you in the face that yes, you want out— you can *always* rationalize away the decision on the basis of timing. This is kicking the can down the road and increases the pain. The reality is that there will never be a *good time* to end a relationship, because life is unexpected in its tragedies and its blessings. What if you finally work up the courage and their mom dies? What if they just got fired from their job? What if they just got into their dream school and you don't want to ruin their happiness?

There is only so much we can do to protect each other from the pain of loss and change. People will get hurt in break ups. Even if it's amicable, it is not easy. But so is staying with someone who you cannot fully love, knowing deep in your heart that you want—*need*—something else. There is never perfect timing, and we will always hurt each other. Accepting this is necessary.

The best we can do is try mitigating the painful impact of a break up rather than procrastinate the decision to leave, hoping for perfect circumstances, all while the attachment deepens. This requires compassionate, honest communication. It could include sorting out logistics of the transition. One of the things I did with my break up was try and help my ex find housing before I left. We lived in an absurdly expensive area, and it was one of my biggest points of guilt; it was a reason I justified staying. I was able to help him find a lead on housing that ended up working out for him.

I flew out and spent a week with him packing up the apartment. We cried together, we held each other, we took many days to grieve the relationship together. We were open and honest, and we celebrated the love that we shared through reminiscing. We supported each other in accepting that our story had finished. Obviously not everyone will have a break up with such a dynamic, but the point is you can break up with grace. It is possible to leave with love, even in the pain of loss.

Rebuilding is inevitable

I cannot promise it will be easy, but you can choose it. Breaking up with someone is merely a choice to lose what will be lost one day anyway. It is an active decision to pursue a new direction, and you will find your way. So will they. The relationship has its own set of challenges, sure, and a break up will bring new ones—but if it is a craving for freedom you cannot shake, if you cannot feel the fullness of love that you know you could, you have permission to let go. If you feel existentially caught, if you've tried to make it work, or even if you haven't yet but you have the intuitive sense that *this is not right*—honor it.

On the other side of this decision, I realize that I dramatized it way too much. You just read my writings. They are soaked in extremely intense emotion. I was so overwhelmed by my feelings, and while I believe finally letting myself fully experience them enabled me to make this decision, I catastrophized the idea of leaving J for years. Leaving J literally seemed like it would be the end of the world, something I could not recover from.

Eventually, I would have lost J anyway. This was something that did not occur to me until after I had chosen to let go. I would have lost him not because it was inevitable that he would leave me, for example, but literally because death would come eventually. It could have taken him before it took me. At that point, I would have to rebuild my life, just as I must do now.

We will always eventually need to rebuild the life that we created with someone, because it will always break down under the destructive force of loss, whether one of us chooses to let go, or death requires us to. In the case of death, we are forced to undergo that change, no negotiation, no promise of a real goodbye. It would be its own unique type of pain. Death requires active participation in a tremendous, frankly unimaginable change. Could you rise to the occasion then? Yes, there is hardly any other choice.

Now, if you *know* in the core of you that you want to break up, you will find the strength to rebuild your life. So will they. You can let go now. You can start over again now. This is the nature of things: choice, change, and consequence.

Never believe you are trapped. Never believe you are not strong enough to forge a new path. And never believe that the other person is not strong enough, either. You have no idea what either of you are capable of—and you also have no idea what great blessings are waiting on the other side for you both. The reality of the human build is that we are highly, brilliantly adaptable creatures. Loss is always a new beginning, and we can find the fortitude to create anew. We are literally made for it.

The clearing

One of my more magical-thinking-based convictions is that, if you intuitively sense some new circumstance is meant for you, it will never arrive nor flourish until you fully clear out whatever stands in its place. In this case, a relationship. You have to be willing to let go of a sure thing to create space in your life for what will actually fit.

This is part of how I believe fate works in tandem with free will. One of the clearest examples of this is in my friend's life. A while ago, she left a terrible relationship where she was mistreated and deeply undervalued. She poured her soul into trying to make it work, but eventually decided she could no longer take the feeling of not being good enough for her partner. It took her a *long* time to make the decision; it was terrifying to let go of a sure thing, even if it was so clearly not for her, and actively antagonistic to her own flourishing.

Once she finally made the choice to end the relationship, a new opportunity for love almost immediately presented itself. It was with a person who she already was somewhat acquainted with, but did not have romantic feelings for. But once she had the room in her life, the relationship organically emerged. Almost two years later, that new relationship has still endured. It is what she wanted all along, and it was not always easy; it challenged her to grow in ways that made her more secure and whole in herself. The firmer her own identity has become, the more intimate and enduring the relationship has gotten.

And, the more she detached from the original relationship she left—ending contact with him completely, giving back belongings, sorting things through with his family, taking care of legal concerns—circumstances of the relationship became more secure. This was not due to the new guy knowing anything had changed for her; she did not confide in him about these things. It always just seemed to unfold naturally.

It seems like a law of intimate energetics. The ultimate depths of romantic love cannot take root and flourish while other attachments to what does not fit are still present. When there is a state of energetic uncertainty, or one storyline has not yet achieved completion, energetic momentum cannot sufficiently build up to actualize a new storyline. It is like the concept of blocking one's own blessings, I suppose.

Both my friend and I knew our relationships were not "it," but we were terrified to let go of them. In my case, I was so afraid to let go of J because it was safe, a sure thing, stable enough and satisfying enough because it was comfortable. We laughed, we mostly did not fight, and so on. But obviously it hit a point where this gnawing sense that *there is something else out there for me* overpowered my denial, and I had to break up.

Prior to our ending, I tried to find what I was looking for in our open relationship while still retaining my relationship with J. Because he told me he could not provide the type of romantic connection I wanted, I tried to find other romantic connections. But those things were never it. They never could be it. For one, I chose some real duds to pursue. But I think whatever awaits simply could not find me. Not only was I not ready as an individual, there was simply no room for it to take root in my life. I needed to sever my tie with J. I yearn for a committed, deep, and ultimately monogamous love. Given that, it is no wonder I would never have been able to find the connection. (And by the way: Please dear God do *not* try an open relationship if you know what you need is to end the relationship. It is not worth the heartbreak. Do not do it. Take responsibility for your desire and own the risk of leaving. This is my biggest regret of all.)

I believe it is not until something is finally, fully complete, once it is set firmly in stone that *there is no going back*, that circumstances will finally align enough for the new relationship to materialize. And that's primarily what I mean—it's about circumstances that are beyond one's own control. This, to me, is the work of God. Once you make the choice to fully let go, take a huge leap of faith, and surrender to the risk of utter failure, some great force can take over and lead you towards what is truly meant for you. And when I say *meant for you*, I don't necessarily mean it is the exact thing you consciously desire. It is not a practice in personally manifesting; it is a practice in personal choice, yes, but the choice to surrender your will to a narrative progression greater than your own will could write, and welcoming in what new story is yours to live out, even if it looks nothing like what you expected.

What if I can fix it?

The eternal quandary: Can I stay and make it work, or is it time to give up completely? It's a really difficult call. Have you *tried* making it work already? Have you had challenging conversations and communicated about the issues that are driving you apart? My general perspective is that, if you really love someone, and you have compatible future goals, it's worth *trying* to communicate through and make compromises to salvage a relationship. But have you *been* doing that for a long time, and it's still not working? In that case, it may be time to say goodbye.

And if you are working on improving a relationship to avoid a full break up, it is important to be honest with yourself about if anything has improved, and what that improvement actually means. In my case, I would think my relationship improved when I successfully quashed my romantic desire and convinced myself the passion I needed was basically a pathological fantasy. That is not actually an improvement, nor a fix. That was me lying to myself to stabilize the relationship, and by extension, the rest of my life. Did it keep the relationship intact? Yes, for eight years. But it came at the expense of my happiness and development (personal and professional), and my ability to envision the future I actually *want*, nevermind actively building it.

If what you need is your partner to make measurable improvements, like changing dynamics about household responsibilities, then maybe that is something that can be improved. It is an actionable request with immediately evident change. But if it's something like a fundamental personality incompatibility, a clash of vision for the future, a pattern of deception and unaccountability...can that really be *fixed*?

Can you really make that work? I mean, maybe. Humans can adapt to all kinds of awful situations and survive. You *could* adapt to a relationship where your boyfriend is cheating on you. You could, for example, just *ignore* it and try to manage your feelings of jealousy, betrayal and insecurity through avoidance and denial. But why *would* you?

It ultimately boils down to whether you are willing to risk a mediocre-to-bad sure thing that has no signs of improvement (the relationship) for a guaranteed uncertain thing (singledom) that actually has potential to become great (a future relationship).

Can you handle uncertainty? Don't answer that, let me answer it for you: Yes. You actually can. We all can, it's built into us, even if it's extremely challenging at first. You will adjust and adapt to a new life, new patterns will emerge, you will settle into new rhythms and habits, and with the risk comes opportunities that you simply would never have in the partnership.

Do not open the
relationship

Do not open the relationship. Do *not* open the relationship. *Do* **not** open the relationship.

There is no such thing as a good time

I kept deferring this break up. I'd message my friends at least once a year for many years of the relationship and say, *I think I need to end this.* The reasons I cited were all those that ultimately led to the demise of the relationship. They were immutable dynamics, ones I tried again and again to accept.

We had many opportunities to naturally end the relationship: When I left for Germany 2 months after we got together, when I got back from Germany, when he graduated college, when he moved for his career, as soon as I left to move back to Connecticut. These were transition points where saying goodbye would have made sense.

It is hard for me to say rationally that *I wish we had done it sooner,* even though I often feel that way. In reality, if I hadn't gone out to California, I would have missed out on more than I can outline. There were people I met who completely changed the course of my life and led me to my Catholic conversion. I don't think I would have written or been so active online the way I was; all of the opportunity that emerged from my anti-cancel culture era may have never come to pass. I am grateful we stayed together, ultimately, but it can be tempting to think *We both could have found this freedom so much sooner.* It can be tempting to spiral out that way as a woman on the cusp of 30, fertility waning.

I am torn between impulses for offering advice on the topic of deferral. On the one hand, as I've written elsewhere, I want to emphasize that there is no perfect time. We *had* "perfect" time—natural transition points—and we did not take them. The timing of the actual break up was logistically bizarre. The need to break up simply hit a point of no return and could no longer be procrastinated or ignored. We had talked about waiting to reconsider this until he had news about whether he'd get a job or not. Once we knew where J would be the next year, I would decide if I wanted to come with him. Ultimately, we could not wait that long. The decision came sooner than expected.

On the other hand, though, given what I experienced, I know that holding out can actually end up bringing you tremendous blessings outside of the relationship, like what I found in my time in Santa Cruz. Sometimes there is a purpose to waiting, even when you *know* in the core of you that you want it to be over. The issue is in the deception. Do you tell them you're thinking about it? What if they believe you have a solid future together, but you're holding out for an opportune time to drop the bomb? Can you live with yourself? Is it fair to them to be deceived?

Ultimately, I suppose my advice is to hone your discernment of timing that exists in a will greater than your own. It is hard for me to separate my spiritual beliefs from this topic. My decision to leave followed my religious journey. I followed signs that reflected back what I already knew, that led me to places where I could remember myself, reconnect to love and God, and finally find the courage to risk leaving my security and being utterly alone. If all signs are pointing towards you getting out, heed them. This is the interplay of fate and free will: If there is a new phase of life past this decision point, the onus is on you to make the choice. Destiny awaits, if only you choose to accept it.

Growing

The phone call

It is Tuesday, July 18, 2023 at 11am. J and I decided to go no contact and see how the other was doing down the line. Today is our six month check-in. Before the phone call, I am filled with dread, as well as immense guilt. I dread that he may still want me, and I feel guilty that I have fully, completely moved on from my attachment to him, almost effortlessly. I felt the pain of my own loneliness, but I did not *miss* him for very long. I did not reminisce or pine. No part of me longs for him, nor misses the life we shared. I feel awful for this, but it is what it is, and I cannot change it.

I still feel guilty about our relationship itself. My best friend constantly reassures me: *You don't have to feel guilty anymore. You did the right thing, once you finally admitted you would never be happy with him and you needed something more, you left. This was the best thing you could have done for him. Stop dwelling on it.*

He asks if I want to FaceTime, and I agree to it. My dread deepens reading that he says it would be nice to see me. When we connect, he smiles earnestly, as is his way, and says, "It's really nice to see you." I feel disgusted with myself, like when someone you've been gossiping about is really kind to you, as if you're carrying a spoiled secret in your stomach. I tell him it's nice to see him too, and in a way it is, but mostly it feels strange. For someone I spent so long with, he feels so unfamiliar, so very much not *mine*.

We exchange life updates, and I am thrilled to hear his career updates. It is the good news I was hoping for. He expresses encouragement of my own plans, the achievements I've made this year, the projects I'm working on. We are supportive of each other. The conversation is casual, pleasant. Then, halfway through the call, he asks me, "Have you had any romantic success?"

I reluctantly confess a strange set of relational circumstances that have emerged over the last six months. It is nothing formal, or even necessarily promising, but it is *something*. It is an unexpected situation, at least in its timing. I ask him if he has had any success himself.

He responds with hesitant excitement. He has found someone. It was unexpected. The timing was not ideal, but they are making it work. They are going to Europe for two weeks together next month. He seems to be trying to withhold gushing, but we both end up gushing a bit anyway. He seems like a more comfortable version of himself, more relaxed, more steady.

He tells me a bit about his new girl, and exclaims, "Turns out I *am* a romantic! I didn't realize I could feel like this about anybody!"

"I knew it! I knew you could, just not for *me*. I'm finally able to see that my problem in our relationship wasn't that you weren't doing enough for me, it's that I...I didn't actually have romantic feelings for *you*. It was an issue of my desire."

"We should have done it sooner. I mean, we did it when we did it, but...we knew. Long before it was over, we knew. We knew in Ireland, don't you think?"

"Yeah. I wish we did it sooner too."

We both express relief. *I felt so guilty, like I moved on so quickly, like I betrayed you.* We reassure each other, exchange apologies for various dynamics, express gratitude for other dynamics, and wish each other lives of beauty and success.

It's so over

The call was overtly positive. It was pleasant and easy. It was genuinely nice to hear from him. I hung up feeling happy, but then something darker settled in. *I am alone now.*

There is no going back; there is no second chance. The life I was living for the last eight years is fully, entirely over. I do not have a fantasy safety net. I never did anyway, but in some selfish corner of my mind I know I must have maintained a cushioning hope: *If this doesn't work out, I can go back. I'm not truly alone.* No, I am alone. I do not have someone who I can run back to, who will embrace me and say *I hoped you would come back.* I did not really want that, I did not expect he wanted that, but over the last six months, the door remained slightly open. I do not want him, and now, I know, without room for delusion or doubt: J does not want *me.*

The selfish, fearful belief that kept me in the relationship for so long has been obliterated by reality. I used to think *No one else could love me like J does.* Now, even J does not love me. In fact, what he has come to realize, he was never truly in love with me. The comfort of habitual safety, of a love based on the choice of companionship, is no longer an option. I am *alone*, absent of romance or companionship.

The full length of the life ahead of me appears infinitely more arduous than it did when I woke up this morning. I look out my window and notice my vision seems crisper, but dimmer. The weight of the world is heavier and my body is denser. I feel the air on my skin; I sense myself in space, and it is only me, and I am fully alive, and I am not just a mind, but a body, and it is only mine, and no one else's is mine to hold. There is no plan B that will ensure a life lived without loneliness—not that I was without it in my relationship anyway. J was never consciously my plan B, but I see now that our relationship settled into my bones that way. It was an existential security blanket, one that seemed immovable. Such a belief is irrational and self-serving, but many beliefs are precisely that: selfish illusions that maintain a merely familiar, yet often soul-crushing, homeostasis.

Every choice is mine, each comes with consequences I will bear alone. There is no future guaranteed to me. There is no love I am promised, owed. I have friends and family, but no partner, no one who I can call home. This has been true for six months already, but now it is unambiguously, unavoidably clear.

I broke up with J in January, and, well, it felt like J broke up with me in July.

I send Discord messages to my college best friend. I send voice messages to my Irish best friend. I Snapchat my childhood best friend. I have received much reassurance from each of them throughout all of this, and they give it again in this new wave of change. They encourage me to continue pursuing the goals I've set for myself. Perhaps it is just that my body is alone; with my friends, my heart is not.

I tell my best friend, the world's most skilled internet sleuth, about my ex's new lover. She quickly locates a photo of her. My jaw drops. It is her, the one from the Instagram post in May, where I had an inexplicable intuition: *They're in love.* So they were, it seems. I pray theirs is the one that sates and stays.

Raw fury

I'm so fucking angry and I can't tell where in my body it begins or ends. It doesn't feel physical. It feels mental and verbal, like I just want to rant and yell. I don't want to punch or hit, I want to scream to the open air or a captive audience and I don't want anyone to contradict a word of what I say. I don't want anyone to tell me to consider a different perspective. I do not want comfort, I literally want a nod and an "I understand." I don't even want that, maybe. Maybe I just don't want to talk to anyone.

I want to hide in the woods and fucking rage and scream and cry until I'm completely empty, nothing left but myself. Actually myself. No apologizing, no diminishing, no fucking gaslighting myself, no self-deception, just pure unadulterated honesty, just absolute fury at how being beaten down when I was young, then being sick, led me to settle for circumstances and opportunities that never satisfied. I am furious with my own choices, that I half-heartedly devoted myself to someone else's life at the expense of creating something for myself, because I no longer believed in my dreams. I invested in a security that never existed, that was destined to disintegrate, that I didn't even truly *want*. I didn't have dreams of my own anymore. I stopped dreaming, and so I stopped doing, I just lived on autopilot and stifled impulse, followed the lead of someone else whose destination was never mine. I floated through life.

I have spent a decade believing so much of my own bullshit. Such delusion, self-deception. I didn't want the future I invested in, second fiddle to a career that wasn't mine, to my fucking illness, and now this narrative irony: He found his before I found mine. I am happy for him, and who knows what the future is, and I haven't been looking anyway, but the *narrative*. The *irony*. What I left for, he found so soon. It is not a race, but I am consumed by the sense that there is a dramatic irony that feels cosmically absurd and spiritually agonizing. My entire mind is wired to seek patterns and write narrative and this one is existentially absurd, overwhelming and right now, infuriating. I wrote these delusional things, I got fixated on these fools and was a fool myself and if I had been honest, or more brave, or if he had realized what he wanted, if we both pulled our weight, it all could have been avoided. I made my relationship a sacred cow that in the secrecy of my mind I slaughtered. Enough.

I regret it. I regret all of this. I resent my past decisions, not just this relationship, the choices within, before, even after it. I resent myself for not having more strength of will, or sobriety, or connection to God. I resent the abuse that led me to believe I was terrible and worthy of suffering, that I would never amount to anything. I resent the selfish men who have used me. I resent the women who have burned me at the stake, and the men who did nothing about it. I resent myself for being selfish, entitled, lazy. I have never felt this angry. I don't know where to put it.

There is no villain. There is no *one* to be angry with. I have abandoned myself. The circumstances of my relationship were what they were, and we tried. It isn't even about him. I simply don't feel angry with him, I just feel globally *mad*. I suppose I feel cosmically angry. Why did I have to get sick when I was younger? Why did I have to get hurt when I was younger? God, why didn't you stop me sooner? I can't believe my regret and grief and anger. I can't process it all at once. I can't focus. I can't do anything but fume, try to channel it. It goes nowhere but out my fingertips or my mouth. Nothing pacifies it, but I don't want it to be pacified anyway. I want to scream. I want to believe I am worth more than what I've given myself. I don't want to talk to anyone, unless they want to listen to me rant. I don't want to explain myself. I don't want to justify myself. I don't want to defend myself. I just want to be fucking angry.

I have spent six months in a limbo, still so focused on romantic yearning. I am sick of it. I don't want to think of love right now. I am tired of longing for men who cannot receive me. I need to turn it off for now, I need to re-focus. I don't want to date, nor daydream, nor theorize love. Not now.

I just want friends

I want someone to pick me up and drive me around and scream music at the top of their lungs with me. I consider calling Emily, but she lives half an hour away and it's 10:30pm on a Tuesday. I consider going by myself, but I just drank beer. Why am I drinking beer? I don't even like to drink. I feel so angry, I feel so restricted. Yesterday I fought off the urge to go to Taco Bell and get my old order: Crunchwrap Supreme, sub beef for beans, add potato, make it fresco.

I am so acutely aware of all the ways I've restricted myself, compressed my desires and compartmentalized. I want to do everything that comes to mind, follow pure impulse, but I know this would be an ultimately self-destructive choice. I haven't had fast food in three years. I'm proud of that. It's like sobriety to me. Eating Taco Bell will not make up for a decade of tightly wound self-deception.

For some reason I am thinking about my high school guy best friend. There is something special about having a guy best friend. I haven't had one since then. I never had one in college. Not like him. It was a purely platonic best friendship. We were so close, back to middle school. I remember one day he picked me up and we drove around, and ended up parked in the parking lot of the church down my street, the halfway point between our houses, the same church

I'm now a parishioner of. I haven't been to mass in weeks. I feel so far away from God.

I cried about my high school ex with him. He was calm and patient. He made me feel better, though he could never understand why I kept on with that guy given how much anguish he caused me. There came a point in that relationship where my friends became distant. I was consumed by the relationship, the drama of it, the constant fights and familial complexities. That was my first experience of love before J. It was highly dysfunctional. We both fell into manipulative patterns and major power struggles.

Maybe I'd sing Florence + the Machine in the car. Roll down the windows and scream: *Leave all your love and your longing behind, you can't carry it with you if you want to survive.* Play it on repeat three times, then switch to her song King and scream *I need my golden crown of sorrow / My bloody sword to swing / My empty halls to echo with grand self-mythology.* Maybe I should call Emily. I don't know why I don't. I guess I don't want to bother her. I don't want to explain anything to anyone. I don't want to be in Connecticut anymore.

I want to be somewhere far away with people I don't actually know, but suddenly come into consciousness and look around and realize they're all my best friends. We've all been best friends our whole lives, we never stopped, I never felt heartbreak, I never felt alone. I've been there the whole time, it was just all a bad dream. No one ever lied about me, ostracized me, I never lost my sense of myself. I stayed true to myself, I never got my heart broken and convinced myself I wasn't worthy of love. I never wasted the second decade of my life weaving in and out of sanity, caught in dead end jobs just to pay rent to be in a place for a career that was not mine. I never made the wrong choices.

My Bible dad friend texted me while I was writing this and I bursted into tears. He sent me a selfie of him smiling and asked "How is confession going?" I haven't seen him since January. He just asked if I'd like to catch up soon. More crying. A small grace. I suppose he was my male best friend, just with more complex dynamics, something more paternal than peer. Once we drove to a restaurant together, on his birthday, windows rolled down, scream-singing Les Miserables. I wish I could have that right now. I wonder if he wishes he could have that ever, too. I wonder if he misses me. I miss him right now.

I am starving for friends, but I can't seem to remember how to make them anymore. I don't know where to find them these days. I suppose I'll meet them when I start my career, if I succeed. If. No, *when*. I need to have a radical unmoving fully convicted belief in myself. What else can I do? How else has anyone achieved anything but a firm belief in themselves and their dreams, persistence, support from people who believe in them and I suppose a stroke of good luck.

I told someone in my life *I still can't believe he has a new girl.* They laughed and said *You're still on that?* Yes. It has been one week, and I am still on that, still confronted with how I came out of the relationship without a future of my own. No career. No network. I did it to myself. I made the wrong choices, over and over. I could not ever blame him, but I look at the way of things, and I ended up with the short end of the stick. It's not a competition, it's not a race to the bottom, but I have so much work to do. A lot ahead of me. I wish I could wake up in the passenger side of my best friend's car driving up to Cape Cod. I wish I could have restarted at 25 after I got on the right meds. I don't want anyone to tell me *You learned so much. You were what each other needed at the time. If you hadn't done that you wouldn't have ended up here.* Here? You think I want to be here? That's not comforting. I just need to be angry.

I am so alone. I do not want to be kissed. And I certainly don't want this stupid beer. I want the windows rolled down in the middle of nowhere screaming Let It Go from Frozen, throwing my head back in laughter when our voices crack, admiring the stars whizzing by through a moon roof. I want to be with people who love me. I want them all with me, I want more, I want so much more.

It is a new day

It is the end of July, and I'm so much calmer today. I drank two cups of coffee, which seems meaningless to most people, but there was a time in my life I couldn't drink coffee because I'd have panic attacks so intense I'd bring myself to the ER. Today I savored the caramel flavor and studied. I finally signed up for a study program I found out about a couple weeks ago, and it is proving useful. I'm excited.

I went to a class with 30 others studying for the LSAT. It was fun to learn from and with others. I have a goal and I will chase it, and I have multiple people who are invested in my success. They text me to check in on my progress. They encourage me. They advise me. They are generous with their support, and for one of the first times in my life, I am fully open to receiving it.

I am less angry today but I know it is important to let myself grieve and oh *God* have I been letting myself grieve. I've been letting myself fucking wail, and scream, and do whatever I need to do. I cried in the shower last night and then called one of my best friends. I am lucky I have friends who will let me express my emotions and support me through them all. I do not know where I'd be without my best friends. They are everything to me.

I've learned that you *must* get angry. I remember one of the last conversations I had with my ex before he dropped me off at the airport, I told him, "Let yourself get angry with me if you need to, ok? You can be mad at me, you should be." I think this is advice everyone should follow. Let yourself be mad. If you repressed it, it is good for you to feel it.

It took me six months to get angry. I was soft, no true bitterness. My focus shifted to the future, to my dreaming, or stayed engrossed in the complex dramas that unfolded in my current relationships. But after that call with him, when I was confronted with the gap between his life and mine, his development and my own, something transformed. I became furious at my past self's choices to repeatedly abandon herself. I am angry at the circumstances of my life over the last decade. I think it is only now that the reality of not only the break up, but the relationship's impact on my development, has settled in.

It is through my anger that I am entering a new stage of becoming an independent person. This anger's roots are in my self-worth, which I betrayed. I see now that I *deserved* to make a different choice. I deserved to be honest with myself, and with him, and I never had to doubt that my feelings were real or justified. I deserve to have a career, and to love who I am, and to enjoy my hobbies. I deserve to take good care of myself. I deserve to make choices that strengthen me as an individual. The time for compromise will come when I have a love worth compromising for. For now, I must be uncompromising in service of my own development.

It is my belief that if you are trying to become a strong woman, you do not ice your emotions out. That doesn't work. Instead, you command them, meaning you let them flow and develop the force within yourself to direct them, so they don't get stuck and ruin you. That's the only way I've come to grow at all: Feel everything, do not run away, let it all move through me and then write. Running never works, it just delays, and life is too short to keep putting it off. This is what I am doing.

I will spend an hour every morning dancing theatrically to my self-empowerment Spotify playlist. The songs are more egomaniacal than I'm used to, but I figure I could use that as an external counterbalance to my standard internal self-criticism. Then I'll study, and write, and if I need to sob uncontrollably in the shower at 1am while listening to Mitski or highly dramatic classical music, I'll fucking do it. Why wouldn't I? Feel it all.

My main priority is cultivating my own personal power and harnessing it towards tangible goals that allow me to build a life of my own. What I am slowly coming to understand is that my emotions, as well as my intuition, actually are the source of my power. Coming to fully understand my emotions, master their language and impact, this is how I can actually become the woman I want to become.

I am refusing to prioritize romance right now, even though it is ultimately what I left my relationship to find. I am not ready for it. I needed to unleash that yearning in me to get out. I needed to realize I have a clear vision of what I want. I see it now. It became so vivid I could almost reach out and touch it. I have a strong sense of what I want, when the time comes. But for now, I must keep the vision in the back of my mind, but get down to business and ruthlessly pursue my own goals.

If the romantic who yearns for a great creative love is the part of me that contains the vision for meaning in life, then she needs to be adequately protected. The rest of me must serve her aims without letting her drive my consciousness. She is just the visionary feeler, not the actual creator or doer. If I yearn for a great partnership, one of powerful creativity, I need to have full command over my own power first. I smothered a fire in me. I must fuel it myself and master the force of its burning heat through intentional containment rather than complete extinguishment. I must become fully myself, in possession of my own heart, serving the aims of my yearning through steady progress and fierce determination to achieve ambitions I abandoned out of fear. I must become one before I become two.

Landing

Epilogue

It is here, dear reader, that I admit to you the secret hidden in the story of my post-breakup life: I fell in love with someone new. My self-assured declaration in July that I must focus on myself rather than my yearning was ultimately no match for the romance of exchanging over 250,000 words of correspondence and countless hours of talking with a writer whose mind I admired more than anyone else's. In October, after many months of wanting, we finally touched. It unleashed a deluge of emotion I did not know I had to feel.

For weeks afterwards I had flashes of memories of my life with J in Santa Cruz. The smell of low tide walking towards the boardwalk was so vivid. My bike ride home from work along the river felt like it was an activity of yesterday. It suddenly seemed strange that I could not get into the yellow Honda Fit, drive to the majestic redwoods and wander around for three hours. I craved burritos from Taqueria Michoacán and breakfast sandwiches from Pretty Good Advice.

I wondered if I missed him, but decided the word did not capture my feeling. To *miss* implies a desire to reconnect or return, neither of which I wanted. I realized what I was feeling was grief. I grieved the way he rubbed my back for hours while he read, or watched TV, or scrolled on his phone. I grieved the way I could collapse into him. We never tired of each other's warmth; I used to say we were like otters. Even after we broke up, we spent hours that final week holding each other. I grieved decorating the Christmas tree with him. I grieved solving puzzles and listening through musicals with him. I grieved doing karaoke with him.

I grieved him. I still grieve him. It took almost a year, and I came to believe I'd never feel it, but I grieve him. I grieve us. I grieve his love, and I grieve loving him. I had felt loneliness after my breakup, but I hadn't truly grieved until someone else touched me.

**

Our grocery store in Santa Cruz had a huge squash cart outside. It was a big wooden wagon overflowing with squashes right outside the entrance of the store. All autumn we'd buy little sugar pumpkins from the cart and roast them. They were locally grown and tasted sweeter than candy. When they roasted, the flesh was a bright, deep orange. That's how you knew you got a good one. If you got a yellow pumpkin, you picked wrong. It had to be orange at full saturation, soft and smooth.

We'd get so excited we'd stand over the stove eating them fresh out of the oven, groaning in ecstasy and amazement at how something could taste so good on its own. I'd yell and squeeze him with excitement. I always squeezed him with excitement. Every time I looked at him I'd tell him how beautiful he was—and he was. He stood still under my grasp and smiled, or wrapped his arms around me and squeezed me back.

I drove to Trader Joe's today. I haven't gotten new groceries in a month. I'm working through my pantry and freezer to save money. I saw sugar pumpkins, but there's no way they're the same. I've had nothing like it. Nothing like those, from the big squash cart, grown in Santa Cruz. We'd comb through for the orangest ones. Nothing like those pumpkins. I bought pre-cut delicata squash from Trader Joe's and roasted it as soon as I got home. I dressed it with maple tahini lemon sauce and some pomegranate seeds. Usually I'd add fresh parsley.

It's November now. In a week it will be a year since I moved back to Connecticut. In under four weeks it'll be Thanksgiving. We had Thanksgiving together every year since 2018. I made family-size servings of green bean casserole, stuffing, mashed potatoes, delicata squash, and some of the pumpkins. I loved watching our friends clear their plates. He'd kiss my forehead and tell me how delicious everything was. There wasn't a meal of mine he didn't love. I can't believe that right now, I even grieve his chewing. I can't believe how sweet the pumpkins were. I can't believe I'm really alone. I hope he is happy. I hope she loves him the way he deserves.

**

Starting in 2021, I was coming to a breaking point in my relationship and I needed a way out. I could no longer tolerate my life, but I had spent year after year after year denying that truth to myself. I believed I was making a horrible mistake if I chose to leave, that I was being selfish or crazy. I insisted that staying with him was the only correct choice. I effectively gaslit myself. Simultaneously, somewhere in those eight years I developed the habit of deferring to J in so many matters. He did not demand this of me; I simply came to believe his reason was superior to mine. He was more logical, while I was given to flights of fancy, and so he became my final arbiter.

So then, it makes a certain sense that in order to decide to break up and begin my own life, I needed to defer to a higher authority. By submitting to a force greater than myself, I felt sufficiently empowered to make that decision. If it felt like a command from an all-knowing higher power that I must heed, then I could actually follow through. I needed the grandeur of God, and the hope of a great union, to empower me to finally leave. For so long I felt like I was floating, undirected, uncertain. Then, I felt found, by God, who carried me. And maybe that's true, if not metaphysically, at least psychologically.

God is not at the forefront of my life right now, although I still cry out to him in my grief. I pray the rosary and find strength in the recollection of climbing Croagh Patrick, the holy mountain in Ireland, which took post-COVID endurance that I sincerely credit to God's grace. Partly my decrease in religious devotion is due to choice—I haven't been to mass in months—but also my psychology has shifted. I mourn more than I yearn. Whatever daydreams once moved me have faded. I don't feel driven to write romantic prose. I'm certainly not dating.

I don't know if I've got a creative partner waiting for me out there in this vast world, but I don't really care right now. I chased that dream to singledom, then into a new love with a man I really thought might be *it*, and then into heartbreak deeper than any other I've felt. The story no longer compels me.

There was an emotional, spiritual adolescence I needed to go through over the last year that makes up much of the personal narrative in this book. It was often defiant, fanciful, and, frankly, self-absorbed. It sought a counter-balancing sense of freedom and possibility. I think this is necessary when moving on from a break up. It is part of a natural individuation process that must occur in order to grow. In my emotional hubris I thought because I had finally achieved such strong certainty in my decision to break up, and because I had truthfully wanted the relationship to end for so long, I had fully *moved on* and was therefore ready to run full speed towards new love. I was not. I instead crashed into grief.

I am no longer floating, nor do I feel carried towards some great hope by the grace of God. If I was carried at all, it seems I have since been placed down, feet firmly on the ground. I like to believe God is still with me, but it is less of an urgent conviction than it is a quiet pleading. Through heartbreak, I have landed, and now I *truly* am alone. I have friends and family, yes, but no physical companionship, nor intellectual, nor emotional. There is no guaranteed person, real or imagined, with whom I can create a future.

My romantic vision may never come to pass, but I am grateful I chose to leave the reality I once lived. It took years to build up the courage, and I know, even in moments of lonely anguish, I made the correct decision. I am finally walking towards a vision of my own: a law career, a balanced mind, a beautiful house, a cabin in the woods, exploring nature, and writing. If someone happens to join me, it's by no force of my own. As the Irish memoirists in their County Clare cottage wrote: *Not everyone can be this lucky. It requires two to have the same shared vision.* If it is a future meant for me, luck will find me when it's time.

Molly Frances is a creative nonfiction writer who also dabbles in social commentary and Catholicism. Her previous work includes the chapbook *Vow*, the political zine *Floating*, and a collaborative zine for people with bipolar disorder, *Euthymia*. Molly publishes essays on her two Substacks. Her books and zines can be purchased on her online shop.

Social commentary: mollyfrances.substack.com

Catholic explorations: holymoley.substack.com

Instagram: @molefrances

Shop (URL): mollyis.online